1003842521

S0-DSE-473

Problem–Based Learning In Inclusive Education

	DATE DUE	
OCT 1 6 2003		
JAN 2 7 2004		
FEB 2 7 2004		
MAR - 5 2004		
- 6 AUG 2004		
AUG 2 8 2004		
AUG 2 9 2005		
2 6 NOV 2005		

LEARNING RESOURCE
CENTRE
GRANT MacEWAN
COLLEGE

Donation

Problem-Based Learning In Inclusive Education

ELIZABETH A. JORDAN
University of British Columbia

MARION PORATH
University of British Columbia

JANET R. JAMIESON
University of British Columbia

Prentice Hall Allyn and Bacon Canada
Scarborough, Ontario

LEARNING RESOURCE
CENTRE
GRANT MacEWAN
COLLEGE

Canadian Cataloguing in Publication Data

Jordan, Elizabeth Anne
     Problem-based learning in inclusive education

Includes bibliographical references.
ISBN 0-13-095923-5

1. Problem-based learning—Canada—Case studies. 2. Inclusive education—
Canada—Case studies. 3. Educational innovations—Canada—Case studies.
I. Porath, Marion, 1944– . II. Jamieson, Janet Ruth, 1955– . III. Title.

LB1027.42.J67 2000   371.39   C99-931560-9

© 2000 Prentice-Hall Canada Inc., Scarborough, Ontario
Pearson Education

ALL RIGHTS RESERVED

No part of this book may be reproduced in any form without permission in
writing from the publisher.

Prentice-Hall, Inc., Upper Saddle River, New Jersey
Prentice-Hall International (UK) Limited, London
Prentice-Hall of Australia, Pty. Limited, Sydney
Prentice-Hall Hispanoamericana, S.A., Mexico City
Prentice-Hall of India Private Limited, New Delhi
Prentice-Hall of Japan, Inc., Tokyo
Editora Prentice-Hall do Brasil, Ltda., Rio de Janeiro

ISBN 0-13-095923-5

Vice President, Editorial Director: Laura Pearson
Acquisitions Editor: Dawn Lee
Marketing Manager: Christine Cozens
Associate Editor: Karen Elliott
Production Editor: Andrew Winton
Copy Editor: Karen Alliston
Production Coordinator: Peggy Brown
Art Director: Mary Opper
Cover and Interior Design: Sarah Battersby
Cover Image: Photodisc
Page Layout: Nelson Gonzalez

1 2 3 4 5   04 03 02 01 00

Printed and bound in Canada.

Visit the Prentice Hall Canada Web site! Send us your comments, browse
our catalogues, and more at **www.phcanada.com**. Or reach us through
e-mail at **phabinfo_pubcanada@prenhall.com**.

All cases in the book were prepared as a basis for class discussion rather
than to illustrate either effective or ineffective handling of a situation.

The dedication of this book means something special to each of us.

For my parents, James A. and Elizabeth M. Wilkins; and especially for my husband, John, and my son, Tristan, who have always believed in me.

E.A.J.

For my parents, John Russell (1903-1991) and Jean Browne, and my husband Merv, all of whom provided support and encouragement.

M.P.

To three generations of support: my parents, Pauline M. Jamieson and the late Lloyd E. Jamieson; my husband, Michael Asch; and my children, Daniel and Jordan.

J.R.J.

Contents

Preface

For any classroom teacher the reality of appropriate planning to meet the needs of students who have special requirements goes far beyond the typical special education course most have experienced. One of the more difficult aspects of these courses is providing the opportunity for teachers to encounter situations they would actually face in their classrooms. Many courses use the case studies format; however, this approach tends to lead students to specific outcomes based on an instructor's objectives. The common phrase "to walk a mile in another's shoes" recognizes the inherent value and learning potential of experiencing a real situation first-hand. Our intent with this text is to provide materials that will duplicate as closely as possible the reality of a true inclusive classroom situation. Specifically, this means that the issues and problems are ill-structured, and represent the disorganized and often confusing reality of working with people. There are no leading questions. Instead, teachers must generate their own questions and issues, identifying what is important to their own specific situation.

Since teachers do not work in isolation, the Problem-Based Learning technique allows teachers, pre-service as well as practising, to duplicate the type of collaboration most often encountered in schools. The final "solution" will allow teachers to experience the realities of dealing with ill-structured problems that don't always have the "right answer." Problems also require solutions that conform to the specific legislation in any given province. This means that teachers must work within the constraints of the philosophy, legislation, and reality they will encounter in their communities.

The organization of this text is somewhat different from the usual textbook. Rather than duplicate information that can be obtained from another text or through library research, this book is about problems. These problems were inspired by our own experiences in elementary and secondary classrooms, although the students represented in each chapter are hypothetical and any resemblance to actual persons is coincidental. The professionals and paraprofessionals featured in the problems vary, as they would in any school. Teachers are encouraged to attempt to understand questions and issues from the viewpoint of the various stakeholders involved in the situation, thus reflecting the reality of having to understand and work with individual students with special needs and the range of other persons in their lives (e.g., parents, school administrators, and health professionals). The text has room throughout for notes and comments, since it's our hope that teachers will make this a working document for their own use in the future.

This book is intended for a wide audience and a range of expertise. Since students are placed in the role of classroom teacher we refer to them as teachers, even though they may be in pre-service teacher training, teachers working in inclusive classrooms, professionals in special education who'd like a teacher's view of the issues, or administrators. We have found that the depth of problem resolution varies with the students' experiences. This means that the problems have value to various professionals and paraprofessionals with a wide range of expertise.

Features of the Text

The Introduction describes the Problem-Based Learning (PBL) technique and provides details that will allow teachers to undertake this type of collaborative research. Since the PBL technique is a flexible one, the organization chart for problem solving that we provide is only a suggestion; individual groups may find a more efficient strategy and we have attempted to build that reality into the directions.

The "chapters," each focusing on an individual student, reflect specific file folders such as would be found in a counsellor's office or on a teacher's desk. When teachers plan for meeting a student's needs they usually start a file. These files are compiled from various sources: informal observations, formal assessments, letters from parents, notes from counsellors, letters from psychologists, etc. They usually contain school and district forms that allow for uniformity of information across a district. In most cases pre-service teachers never have access to these forms until they're either given one to fill out or encounter one when dealing with a specific student. In this book the file folders are representative of the type of material a teacher would experience in any school district.

The range of issues teachers need to consider in inclusive classrooms is usually broad and complex, and we've attempted to represent this reality within the files. While some files appear at the start to be straightforward, we've found that the complex reality of dealing with individual pupils quickly surfaces. Each file includes a range of student needs and school/community issues. The focus of work within each file will depend on the intent of the instructor and the interest or the level of expertise of the problem-solving group.

The problems encourage teachers to gain confidence in researching strategies and alternatives for meeting students' needs. By accessing the most recent research through current technology teachers build facility in seeking alternative strategies and new ideas.

The Bibliography includes Web sites that provide a starting point for accessing information. Specific journals are listed as a starting point for resource materials. Space has been left in the Bibliography to note other electronic addresses as they are found.

Text Organization

Since the focus of this text is on the student and not on a categorized label, the files are organized according to student names. Thirty-five files cover the elementary and secondary years, including students in transition from preschool to kindergarten, elementary to secondary, and secondary to vocational/work.

Each file is organized into two parts. The first is a scenario providing a framework from which to view an issue or problem. Because the intent is to provide the student with special needs with as inclusive a classroom setting as possible, each situation considers the needs of the classroom teacher. The second part is the actual file, which contains material relevant to the questions about the student's particular needs. This information ranges from pertinent art work to formal assessments. In many instances the classroom teacher is an integral part of the school-based team and needs to have facility in interpreting sometimes complex and/or conflicting information.

Wide margins are left to encourage notes and comments, since this type of material lends itself to side notes. The text is meant to be written on as ideas, strategies, interpretations, and comments develop.

The Instructor's Manual and the text are integral components of this PBL approach to inclusive education. Not only does the text contain background information regarding the Problem-Based Learning technique, but it also includes a number of ideas on presentation, implementation, and evaluation. The flexibility of the material for course use is emphasized in the Instructor's Manual.

Acknowledgments

Works such as this represent the support of many people, both in terms of ideas and encouragement. For all of these people's efforts we are very grateful. They have given us their time, energy, and enthusiasm because of their commitment to meeting the needs of all children. Very special thanks to each person individually:

Shane Barclay, M.D.

Gillian Bickerton

Marielle Flynn

Ruth Stewart

John Robert Esliger

Judith Duffield

Scott Grabinger

Iris Schneider

Meghan Porath

Jacqueline Kupu

Anne C. Page

Travis Page

Victoria Page

Art More, Ph.D.

M. Cay Holbrook, Ph.D.

Penelope Bacsfalvi

In addition, we would like to acknowledge the contributions of students in our courses who responded enthusiastically to this approach to learning. We discovered that the PBL approach is an enriching and energizing experience for all concerned. To all of those students, thank you for the questions you asked, the issues you raised, and the insights you demonstrated. They provided the intellectual challenge that resulted in this text.

Finally, we would like to acknowledge the following reviewers, whose suggestions have contributed to the development of this book: Sheila Bennett, Brock University; Cheryl Duquette, University of Ottawa; Judy Lupart, University of Calgary; Dona Matthews, Ontario Institute for Studies in Education; and Elizabeth Starr, University of Windsor.

Problem-Based Learning In Inclusive Education

I hear and I forget
I see and I remember
I do and I understand.
—Confucius

Introduction

Problem-Based Learning is an extension of Bruner's (1960) theories that people learn when challenged to discover, to stretch ideas beyond memorizing mere facts or heuristics, and to actually apply thinking skills and knowledge to solve everyday problems. In daily situations people manipulate information; they translate concepts into their own words, critically analyze ideas, discuss and debate among colleagues, integrate concepts across disciplines, acquire new insights, explore variations, and finally give the best idea a try. In other words, people actively grow and learn in an environment that encourages interaction and communication with colleagues in a real situation.

A Brief History of Problem-Based Learning

The transition from understanding how people learn to classroom application occurred in the early 1970s, when McMaster University in Ontario developed a problem-oriented medical program. The University found that there was a difference between memorizing factual knowledge and implementing it in situations with real patients. Students moved from a traditional, isolated, memory-oriented learning style to a mutual, group-oriented, solution-finding learning style. The students found that asking the right questions was often as important as the answers obtained, and sometimes more important. Expert physicians identify a problem and its solution by the kinds of answers patients give to the questions asked. The application of knowledge to actual problem solving became a goal for the medical school. The emphasis was on the use of meaningful information to determine a patient's problem and formulate treatment. Classes changed from lecture formats to small group discussions, where the instructor became a tutor rather than a dispenser of knowledge. The success of that program caused this technique for learning to expand, first within medicine, then across disciplines. Problem-Based Learning has become an effective tool in a wide variety of fields, providing an authentic learning experience in a multidisciplinary format.

A Brief Philosophical Framework
for Problem-Based Learning

While for many programs Problem-Based Learning appears to be a "new" way of approaching a subject field, it's actually based on several respected philosophical frameworks. By briefly pointing out the underlying basis for this technique teachers can readily see the efficacy of this approach.

Problem-Based Learning is predicated on the Constructivist theory that learners construct knowledge based on experiences. Within this theory, according to Catherine Twomey Fosnot (1996), the learning process is

> viewed as a self-regulatory process of struggling with the conflict between existing personal models of the world and discrepant new insights, constructing new representations and models of reality as a human meaning-making venture with culturally developed tools and symbols, and further negotiating such meaning through cooperative social activity, discourse, and debate (pp. ix).

Semantic knowledge, such as mathematical knowledge or social knowledge, is then stored in inter-related networks that expand and become richer as new information and experiences are added. As these concepts grow different ideas inter-relate, causing variations on interpretations (Fogarty, 1997; Gijselaers, 1996). When learners then encounter new problem situations they retrieve relevant information, seek more knowledge about the situation, expand their content and conceptual background, and eventually find the best solution (given the circumstances of the problem).

The traditional "case study" approach to learning focuses on specific questions about topics that have been chosen by the instructor. Learners tend to answer the questions asked with very little, if any, expansion beyond the selected topic. Problem-Based Learning, by contrast, is structured on the tie between the university classroom and reality. By using real problems, teachers are placed in situations that prepare them for what they'll encounter when they begin their careers. Not only is the problem real but the environment for solving it is also real (Newmann & Wehlage, 1993; Stepien & Gallagher, 1993). Teachers work in small, cooperative groups, and knowledge is constructed through interaction with peers. Group discussions allow for the addition of new information, a variety of interpretations, and the manipulation of knowledge. John Dewey (1933) called this Experiential Learning. It's the reality of the situation combined with peer interaction that allow us to truly experience a problem.

Everyday Problems

Problems in real life are usually ill-structured. That is, aspects of the information needed to solve problems are often missing, or the problems change over time. Unlike traditional school problems that are designed to teach a concept and yield a specific or, more commonly in education, a correct answer, ill-structured problems are often difficult even to define. Answers tend to be open-ended and change with the people involved and/or the situation. Because we continually encounter these types of problems we build a repertoire of responses that allow us to function with few interruptions in everyday living. We don't see these situations as problems because we've learned from communicating with others how to respond, or we've learned the hard way how to react to a situation or person.

In other words, our understanding of what constitutes a problem depends entirely on whether we can readily respond to it. For instance, the first time we use public transportation we need to acquire knowledge (bus schedules) and to plan (how long to get where we're going). Once knowledge is gathered it can still be variable (the bus doesn't come on time) and require consultation to solve the dilemma (asking other people at the bus stop about alternative routes). However, once we have some experience with the situation we learn to adapt to the variables that occur in life and we no longer consider the situation a problem. Thus, it is experience with ill-structured problems that allows us the opportunity to develop critical thinking and coping skills.

Solving Ill-Structured Problems

Ill-structured problems require a different approach than is traditionally encountered in education. Solving the problem becomes an active, dynamic endeavour. Unlike case studies, where students are given specific questions to direct their learning, problem-based learning investigations are open-ended, with the students charting the direction. All the problems presented in this text are in a format that may be encountered within an elementary or secondary school by a classroom teacher. Each situation begins with an introduction to the environment and a classroom problem from the teacher's perspective. The student folders contain information either requested by the teacher or given to the teacher for planning purposes. Final solutions are usually the "most preferred decision" by a group rather than an attempt to find the "right" solution.

School–Classroom Environment

In the school and the classroom we encounter the same types of ill-structured, everyday problems that are found in all other aspects of life. And in order to understand the problems found within this text, it's important to clarify the environment in which they occur.

All schools and classrooms are composed of a unique, interactive group of people working toward a set of common goals, as well as a set of individual goals. Within each individual is an overall driving expression of personality shaped by a background composite of family and society. Depending on the background of each individual the composition of the class may vary, sometimes from one day to the next. Teachers will often mention how differently a class "works" when one or two students are absent. This substantiates the fluid nature of any given classroom. Each student provides a personal energy that influences how the class approaches a lesson and how well that lesson is received. Secondary teachers in particular are always stymied when the same lesson, given two periods back to back, works for one group but not the next. The reason is usually the unique composition of each class.

On the next level of the class–school composite are the teachers and the administrators. Their own individual backgrounds are overlaid with philosophies, teaching styles, social-cultural awareness, etc. Also, we need to take into consideration biases, both rational and irrational, which everyone possesses. In many instances they may subtly influence behaviour without the person realizing it. All these influences meld with the composite of student personalities to produce a particular classroom environment. These individual classes combine under an administration to form a school environment. Reciprocally, this environment gives each class and each school a uniqueness that is very evident to visitors.

This complex interaction of people and personalities is important, in that the concept of variability helps to refine our understanding of why some actions or events are problems in one situation but not another. It helps to explain why:

- Variations occur even in such areas as basic educational definitions. For example, in some school districts the term "Inclusion" may mean that schools support selected pull-out programs, while in other districts there may be a policy that all support must be done in the home classroom. Even individual communities may support one type of program but not another based on the inherent philosophies of that community.

- One teacher may view a student as having a learning problem while another teacher, given the same set of experiences with the student, perceives the problem to be one of motivation. The "solution" to any problem is always driven by the analysis of the problem (an important point to remember in any critical analysis). This is often a source of frustration when opposing viewpoints need to be considered. Since teachers don't work alone in a school, understanding and collaboration are important.

- Difficulties sometimes occur when parents feel they are observing some type of problem with their child that isn't perceived by the teacher. In the past few years a growing number of parents are having their children assessed privately by educational psychologists, usually because the parents feel that the school is not identifying some critical learning problem. These reports are then presented to teachers and administrators, with varying results, since if the teacher doesn't honestly view the situation as a problem then his or her solution may not be as effective as the parent anticipated. This emphasizes again the need for a collaboration to produce a joint, initial understanding and defining of the problem.

- Many school districts feel overwhelmed by the number of names being submitted for assessment of learning problems. In trying to meet the needs of every student the system often becomes overloaded. Budgetary demands often prevent hiring more teachers and support personnel. In order to maintain that very fine balance between student needs and budget considerations many viewpoints must be considered. This may be difficult, given the inherent emotional quality of involvement with a particular student and the desire to enhance his or her success.

- Consideration must be given to all points of view—including that of the student, who is one of the most overlooked individuals. Often we need to be reminded that, as adults, we'd be insulted if someone took it upon him or herself to make decisions that would affect our future without consulting us. And yet in many instances teachers and administrators do exactly that. The issue of whether or not to include the student's opinion or viewpoint becomes even more important as the student enters secondary school. With the exception of very young children, or those students who are unable to participate in the planning process, all students should be part of the planning for their future.

The problems in this text attempt to provide the variation that is prevalent in all schools. By acknowledging the range of ideas and variability in the classroom, teachers using this text will get a more accurate, realistic problem-solving situation.

The Goals of Problem-Based Learning

The goals of the Problem-Based Learning technique in inclusive education are:

1. to develop effective problem-solving skills
2. to develop knowledge acquisition and retention skills
3. to develop effective and efficient skills for utilizing knowledge
4. to develop collaboration and communication skills
5. to develop a multiple-perspective problem-solving technique
6. to encourage self-directed and lifelong learning
7. to encourage flexibility and adaptability in teaching style
8. to enhance confidence in teaching ability, specifically regarding students with special needs.

Organizational Steps

The following steps, and the Problem Solving flow chart on p. 7, are suggestions for organizing the problems.

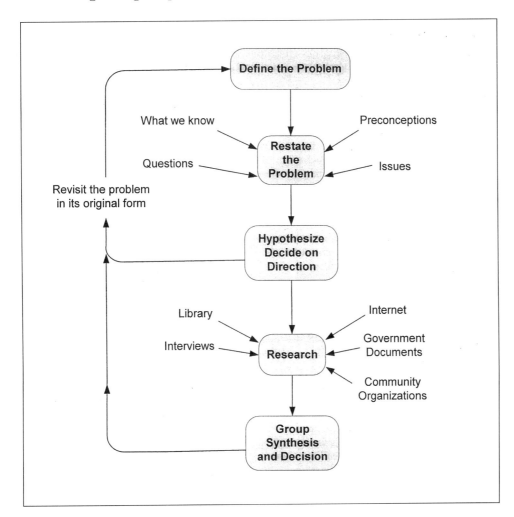

As with anything in real life, variations occur depending on the situation and individuals involved. After working on a couple of problems your group may find more efficient methods of dealing with the various issues. However, we suggest that the elements of organization outlined here form the basis of any problem-solving methodology.

As an additional organizational resource, the Step-By-Step Problem Solving flow chart (McKee, 1995) outlines the various stages used by a school district in planning for a student with special needs. By analyzing this chart you'll see the sequencing necessary for school-based referrals, formal assessments, and preparation of an Individual Education Plan. Knowledge of this process is important, since it provides the context within which most school districts function. Note how this flow chart delineates the process according to the increase in resources needed, and that it is read from the bottom up. This emphasizes the need to keep a balanced view of the district support services available. As mentioned before, budgetary concerns and numbers of students often limit the services available.

For most classroom teachers the area of greatest concern is that identified in the chart as "Recognition of Social and/or Learning Difficulties," which occurs *prior* to Phase I on the chart. Our understanding of the problem-solving process emphasizes that the identification or awareness of a problem is a necessary prerequisite. For many teachers this awareness occurs when they suddenly realize that a student has been having the same kinds of difficulties over and over, that what the student can describe verbally doesn't match her written work, or that the student doesn't seem to catch all of the directions. The problem may only become evident in a phrase, or a single homework assignment. But it's the point at which the teacher understands the need for some type of more individualized involvement. Since it's often a single event or series of assignments that finally makes a teacher realize that there is very definitely a problem, the files in this text reflect those starting points.

The items listed under Phase I on the chart have the greatest relevance for most classroom teachers. For even though teachers may participate in the school-based team or be involved in some types of support situations, it's the actual classroom situation that presents the most concern. The types of situations presented in this text reflect classroom situations. Too often teachers are given the impression that support services—teaching assistants, or testing and evaluation—are readily available, whereas in most schools teachers may have to informally evaluate as well as develop and implement interventions while waiting for the more formal process as outlined on the chart. This reality is most apparent with those students whose needs may not be as evident or critical as those of other students. For example, a student with a learning disability in reading may be able to function in class at a level sufficient to minimally satisfy a teacher or parents; however, the level and quality of work may be far below the student's actual potential. Since such a student is functioning at a minimal level, if the school's resources are already overloaded, he or she may not be considered a priority for special services. While it's hard for a teacher or parent to accept this viewpoint, there are a large number of students who fall into this grey area for identification and assessment—and it is this group that poses the greatest challenge to a classroom teacher. The student may be referred to the school-based team, but it may take some time

PHASE IV: Formal Assessment, reporting, specialized resource
access and coordination and program (IEP)
planning

Formal, written, <u>informed</u> consent (know who, what, why; option to
discontinue, right to hearing)
Often school psychologist is assessment case manager-coordinates
assessment process including assessment by other professions
(speech and language, clinical psychologist, medical specialists),
administer appropriate individualized measures (Level C tests),
coordinate reporting to team and parent, coordinate written report
Assessment by qualified assessment specialists-usually district staff, (may
have been participant in earlier phases or be part of school-based
team) may involve Learning Assistance teacher, School
Counsellor, School Psychologist, Speech/Language Pathologist,
Physiotherapist or Occupational Therapist, other district program
area specialists (e.g., social adjustment, gifted, multicultural,
social work, diagnostic classroom), referral to agencies or
services in the community or other ministries
School-based team makes identification decision (related to funding) and
recommendations for supplementary support services
School-based team develops IEP (with teacher, parent, and student) which
documents goals, strategies and resources to support progress,
responsibilities for implementation, means of evaluating progress,
period of review.

PHASE III: Referral to school-based team

School-based staff who plan and coordinate support services for students
with special needs
Extended consultation on classroom strategies (with minimal support)
Appoint case manager
Referral, access, and planning for other school, district, community, or
interministerial services
Referral for extended assessments (pending parental/guardian consent,
student assent) for identification and planning

PHASE II: Consultation and collaboration, classroom
intervention

Teacher consult and collaborate with school-based resources persons
(administrator, colleague, English Language Centre teacher,
learning assistance teacher, counsellor, child care or multicultural
worker) or resource teams
Observation in classroom and other settings
Additional (level B) assessment - record review, work samples, criterion
referenced testing, informal diagnostic procedures, curriculum-
based assessment, analysis of curriculum and required
prerequisites, assess prerequisite skills, experimental teaching
Develop and implement classroom interventions with evaluation and record
of outcomes
Identify need for further assessment

PHASE I: Observation, Problem Identification, Instructional
Variation

Communication with parent and student throughout all phases
Vision, hearing, screening other health issues by school nurse
With nurse and parent, assess need for other medical assessment
In depth, systematic observation and evaluation of learning needs, current
levels of performance, prerequisite skills
Systematic variation in instructional approaches, teaching techniques,
curricular materials, management techniques
Evaluation of differential outcomes of variations, assess need for
consultation, SBT Referral

FOR THE GREATER NUMBER OF HIGH INCIDENCE LEARNING
AND BEHAVIOR DIFFICULTIES

Increasing Use of Resources →

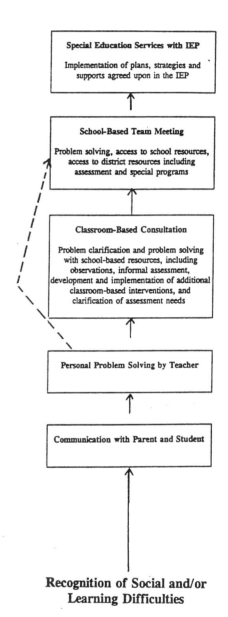

**Step-By-Step Problem Solving
Learning and Behavior Problems**

Special Education Services with IEP

Implementation of plans, strategies and
supports agreed upon in the IEP

School-Based Team Meeting

Problem solving, access to school resources,
access to district resources including
assessment and special programs

Classroom-Based Consultation

Problem clarification and problem solving
with school-based resources, including
observations, informal assessment,
development and implementation of additional
classroom-based interventions, and
clarification of assessment needs

Personal Problem Solving by Teacher

Communication with Parent and Student

**Recognition of Social and/or
Learning Difficulties**

McKee (1995).

before any assessment can be done. In the meantime the student continues to work within the regular classroom, and it's up to the teacher to adapt or modify the curriculum to ensure as much success as possible. It is precisely this type of challenge that we've incorporated into the student files of the text.

As you work through the files in the text this chart will provide information necessary for your planning. For example, the classroom teacher may suggest formal assessment of a student, but this is usually the prerogative of the school-based team, which has access to resources and programs.

Your instructor should provide a timeline within which the assigned problem must be solved. In many cases this will determine whether class time can be devoted to group meetings, or if it can incorporate individual research as well. In any case, it's advisable to determine within your group exactly how you'll divide the time allotted.

Problem-Solving Organization

Define the Problem

While this task may seem to be straightforward and perhaps the easiest, it's actually the most crucial. Research on problem solving shows that how we define problems drives how we solve them (Chi, Glaser and Farr, 1988; Voss and Post, 1988; Wagner and Sternberg, 1986). Every problem contains cues or key elements that we identify as important or that we discard as being superfluous to the issue at hand. If cues are mislabelled in importance, this can lead to an inefficient solution. This means that the problem needs to be looked at from a variety of perspectives: teacher, student, parent, community, social, cultural, educational, etc. Along with these perspectives, make sure to account for the built-in bias every individual brings to any situation. Try to redefine the problem in your own words. Make sure that you revisit the problem in its original form, as well as in the reworded form, as you progress through the solution. Ill-structured problems, especially those involving people, have a tendency to change as the solution progresses. Cues, which were originally excluded, may take on new meaning with added information.

Re-state the Problem

Separate the elements or cues within the problem into areas outlined on the following diagram: what we know, preconceptions, issues, and questions.

What We Know	Preconceptions
Issues	**Questions**

1. *What We Know* includes background information given in the problem that forms the basis for decisions that will be made. This category may also contain information that's already understood by the group and therefore needs no further research, such as a grade equivalent score. Often this information forms the parameters within which any solution must realistically function. For example, an eight-year-old student who rides the bus can't be given extra help after school unless arrangements are made for her to get home safely.

2. *Preconceptions* include all the elements of the problem that aren't understood or fully understood. For example, while the group may know what I.Q. stands for they may feel that more information about the topic would provide a greater insight into the problem. Analyzing the preconceptions

also includes identifying personal assumptions about the student, his or her background, or the environment in which the problem is placed.

3. *Issues* include all of the necessary constraints surrounding the student and/or problem. Issues arise from the variety of perspectives mentioned above and take the form of legal, moral, ethical, emotional, and economic considerations. These must be identified, since they have an impact on the solution and its implementation. For example, there may be a legal issue within a province regarding how late a student may be kept at school, even for extra help.

4. *Questions* include all the items that your group brings up in the discussion as it works on a solution. Initially all questions should be recorded without value judgments. A question that may seem off-topic in the beginning may later provide another avenue to explore. Questioning needs to be ongoing throughout the problem-solving process. Good questions may be more important than the information they yield because they provide a focus and force a synthesis of ideas.

Hypothesizing

As you work through the problem you'll start to have hunches about the solution and what kinds of information would provide more insight into the situation. Record the hypotheses that initially provide the most plausible direction for your group. Decide which direction, or directions, you'll work on as a group. They must be clear to everyone, since you'll be working under time constraints and valuable time will be lost if you work on tangential issues. Assign each person the task of researching and bringing back to the group detailed information on some aspect of the problem as you have defined it.

Researching

During this part of the process each person gathers detailed information on the assigned aspect of the problem. How the information is gathered can be varied. While references are provided in the text, we suggest that individuals consider specialized texts, interviews, the Internet, community organizations, ministry documents, materials from other countries, and related topics.

Group Synthesis and Decision Making

All information is brought back to the group for dissemination and discussion. The group must absorb all of the gathered information; synthesize concepts; exchange ideas; and finally, brainstorm options. The intent is for the group to work in a think-tank format. This isn't the type of assignment where each person does one section in isolation. The entire group is responsible for all parts of the assignment.

Finally, establish a solution that seems the most worthwhile for your group. You may find solutions that are more preferable than others, but these may not be feasible due to constraints beyond your control. A rationale for your solution should include justification for all decisions your group made.

Perspectives

One of the most important aspects of problem solving involves understanding *whose* perspective is being taken when determining a solution. Most situations in this book are presented from the teacher's perspective. However, the teacher is only one person involved in the life of any student. Often a solution that's appropriate for the teacher may not necessarily be adequate for another person or situation. It's necessary to expand beyond the classroom in order to identify as many individuals and situations as possible that may have an impact on either the student's life or the decisions made in a school. The final decision in any of these cases, as in an actual classroom, is the result of a collaboration between the teacher and a wide variety of other individuals.

The Education Community

Each school and district is governed by provincial and federal regulations that identify the legal parameters within which all classroom operations must function. The terminology and duties for specific personnel vary according to regions. It's important to determine the information specific to the region or district in which these problems will be discussed, since that information will constrain the decision. For example, in many instances an Individual Education Plan may not be implemented unless it's approved by the parent. The specific language in which that decision must be expressed may be another factor to take into consideration. For example, the specific education plan for a student may be referred to as either an Individual Education Plan (IEP), Individual Program Plan (IPP), Special Education Plan, or Personal Program Plan.

However, there is a commonality of tasks within education that allows a general overview of the community. In any school a teacher may encounter both certified and non-certified staff involved with the education of a student. The certified staff may consist of reading teachers, learning assistance teachers, school psychologists, speech and language specialists, counsellors, etc. The non-certified staff, or paraprofessionals, may include teacher assistants or special education assistants. The specific roles and responsibilities of these people will vary depending on the job description and/or their training. In general, the paraprofessional is under the supervision of the classroom teacher, who has the legal responsibility within the classroom. Make sure that the tasks and responsibilities of the paraprofessional are clear to everyone in order to prevent any potential difficulties in decision making.

In order to emphasize the necessity for full understanding of roles and responsibilities prior to any decision making, a very brief set of descriptions follows.

Roles and Responsibilities

The teacher is responsible for designing, planning, supervising, and assessing programs for all students in the class. The classroom teacher may require the aid of a Teacher Assistant (TA) to deliver programs to a student with special needs. However, the responsibilities for the special needs student remain with the classroom teacher. The teacher must work with the TA to provide direction in using specific techniques, scheduling parameters, doing IEP-related tasks, arranging resources, understanding various discipline structures, planning content of any home/school communication, and so on. The more communication between the teacher and the TA, along with a collaborative working environment, the more successful the school experience will be for the teachers, the staff, and the students. The teacher maintains the legal responsibility for the education of all students under his or her care.

A Teacher Assistant works with a classroom teacher to facilitate the delivery of teacher-planned programs to students with special needs. The TA works under the classroom teacher's direction to assist a special needs student in becoming more independent and as active a member of the classroom as possible. All instructional and evaluation decisions, as well as communication with parents and other professionals, are the responsibility of the teacher. The TA is not in the classroom to perform duties that could be considered secretarial; i.e., photocopying, filing, and arranging bulletin boards.

Beyond the classroom, the parents or guardians form a vital support service to the student and teacher. Any decisions made about a student must consider the parents' or guardians' perspective. Usually any written education plan must have signed parental/guardian approval. Other community perspectives or resources might include public health, church or religious support organizations, specific ethnic practices, justice system, health and welfare, social workers, medical and paramedical professionals, itinerant teachers, and psychological or behavioural professionals, etc.

All the information input regarding the special needs of a student means that the final decision made by the classroom teacher is a collaborative effort of many people. Often the committee (school-based team) within the school designated to organize an appropriate education plan identifies the individuals involved with the decision making and service delivery. As these people bring their viewpoints to the discussion it will cause a shift or change in the original problem. This is the nature of real life and ill-structured problems.

File 1

Emily

Lynn Jacobs sat at her desk surrounded by files and papers. It was early September and she was beginning the task of familiarizing herself with the incoming Grade 8 students who would need extra support. As the resource teacher for Lakeview High School, one of her responsibilities was to coordinate school-based team meetings. Lynn felt challenged by what she saw in Emily Gordon's file. There was a psychoeducational assessment report done a couple of years before that showed Emily to be exceptionally bright. There were also Emily's reports from elementary school, all of which indicated real difficulties with social relationships. Lynn remembered the long meeting in June.

At the end of each school year, Lynn met with Grade 7 teachers who had students who'd need support in high school. Emily's mother attended that meeting as well. Lynn found out that Emily's success in elementary school was variable. It seemed that she needed a very secure, predictable environment and a supportive teacher in order to do well. Ms. Gordon and Emily's teacher expressed major concerns about Emily's ability to adapt to life in high school. Ms. Gordon said that she'd been Emily's support system throughout elementary school. She clearly was tired and stressed by this, as well as concerned that Emily needed to develop the social skills that would allow her to form good relationships with her peers.

Ms. Gordon, at the suggestion of the elementary school counsellor, had taken Emily to the local children's hospital for assessment over the summer. Emily was diagnosed as having Asperger's Syndrome. Lynn wondered what to do next. She had only a vague notion of what Asperger's Syndrome was and what the implications were for Emily. She reached for the phone and left a message for the district special education consultant.

Eileen Krechinsky, Ph.D.
Registered Psychologist

Suite 111, 97 Ormond Drive

Clear Lake, Manitoba

555-9974

August 10, 1996

REPORT ON THE PSYCHOEDUCATIONAL ASSESSMENT OF EMILY GORDON, AGE 11 YEARS (BD NOVEMBER 21, 1984)

I assessed Emily at the request of her mother, Ms. Alicia Gordon, who wished information on Emily's intellectual and academic abilities to help with educational planning. Because Ms. Gordon expressed concern about Emily's social adjustment, social-developmental assessment was undertaken as well. I met with Emily on two occasions, July 10 and 17, 1996, and with Ms. Gordon on July 31, 1996.

TESTS ADMINISTERED

Wechsler Intelligence Scale for Children—Third Edition (WISC-III)

Woodcock-Johnson Psychoeducational Battery—Revised: Tests of Achievement—Standard Battery

Social Skills Rating System

Self-Perception Profile for Children

Wechsler Intelligence Scale for Children—Third Edition (WISC-III)

Verbal IQ	143	99.79th percentile
Performance IQ	133	98th percentile
Full Scale IQ	136	99th percentile

Observations

Emily's verbal abilities are very well developed. Her level of performance is attained by less than 1% of the population. Her performance on visual-spatial tasks that require the abilities to think in, interpret, and manipulate visual images is at a level achieved by only 2% of the population. Emily's overall performance as indicated by the Full Scale IQ score falls into the very superior range. This level of performance is attained by only 1% percent of the population.

Woodcock-Johnson Psychoeducational Battery—Revised: Tests of Achievement—Standard Battery

Broad Reading	154	99.9th percentile

This score is a measure of reading achievement comprising the ability to identify words (99.9th percentile) and the ability to comprehend what is read (99.6th percentile).

Broad Mathematics	132	98th percentile

This score is a measure of mathematics achievement comprising the ability to do mathematical calculations (82nd percentile) and the ability to analyze and solve mathematical problems (99.6th percentile).

Broad Written Language	141	99.7th percentile

This score reflects achievement in written language. Both applied skills (spelling, punctuation, capitalization, word usage) (98th percentile) and written expression (99.9th percentile) make up the score.

Broad Knowledge   113   81st percentile

This score reflects the achievement of general knowledge in science (97th percentile), social studies (56th percentile), and the humanities (63rd percentile).

Skills   150   99.9th percentile

This score reflects the achievement of general academic skills (decoding, written language, and calculation).

Emily's academic achievement is outstanding, particularly in the core areas of reading, mathematics, and written language. She also demonstrates strong knowledge of science. Her achievement in social studies and humanities, while average, is relatively lower than her achievement in other academic subjects.

Social Skills Rating System

Emily and her mother completed ratings of her social skills using this standardized rating scale. Both Emily and Ms. Gordon rated her overall social skills as below average (8th and 16th percentile, respectively). This overall rating comprises more specific area ratings of cooperation, assertion, and self-control. Ms. Gordon also rated responsibility and Emily rated empathy. Their ratings were as follows:

	Emily	*Ms. Gordon*
Cooperation	Below average	Below average
Assertion	Average	Below average
Self-Control	Below average	Average
Responsibility		Average
Empathy	Average	

On a separate rating, Ms. Gordon did not indicate any concerns about problem behaviours.

Self-Perception Profile for Children

This scale asks children to rate their perceptions of themselves in five areas—scholastic competence, social acceptance, athletic competence, physical appearance, and behavioural conduct. There is also a rating of overall self-worth, indicating the extent to which the child likes him or herself as a person. There is a parallel scale for parents. Ratings done by Emily and her mother are summarized on the graph below.

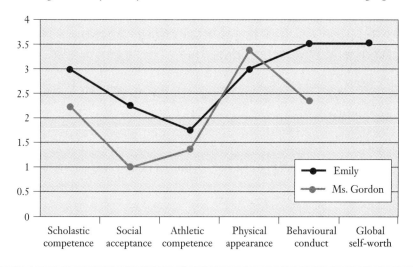

SUMMARY AND RECOMMENDATIONS

Emily demonstrated a number of exceptional strengths in this assessment. Her reasoning abilities and her academic achievement are outstanding. In both assessment sessions, Emily was highly motivated to solve the problems presented to her. In the academic achievement assessment, she often became so engrossed in the activities that she had to be reminded that there were a number of questions to be completed.

Ms. Gordon's concerns about Emily's social relationships are reflected in her ratings of Emily's social skills and social acceptance. Emily also indicated some concern with social skills, particularly cooperation and self-control. She rated her acceptance by others as average. There are some differences between ratings of social behaviours and acceptance. I have suggested to Ms. Gordon that she contact the counsellor at Emily's school about monitoring her adjustment in Grade 7, particularly as Emily will be moving on to secondary school in a year's time.

Emily's academic strengths need to be considered in academic planning. Her curriculum should be matched to her outstanding abilities.

Eileen Krechinsky

Registered Psychologist

File 2

Josh and Jennifer

Laura Webster sat in the sun watching her Grade 1 pupils play at recess. In her three years as a Grade 1 teacher Laura had become used to working hard at the beginning of the year to promote respectful behaviours on the playground. So this September was a treat—this group really got along well together. Laura took the chance to watch her pupils and reflect on their development so far.

Laura's eyes lingered on Josh Cameron—slight, fair-haired, and brilliant. She couldn't believe how much he knew! He stood watching the others from the playground's edge. He seemed so reluctant to join them at play. What was wrong? Was he shy or unsure of himself? He didn't seem so with her. With her, he was so personable, so eager to talk about his favourite books and different ways to do math. He virtually lit up when he talked. And boy, did this kid know dinosaurs! He knew things about natural history she could never hope to master. But here on the playground and in group work in the classroom, he seemed so out of it. How could this be? So intellectual, but so out of it socially.

Laura's thoughts were interrupted as she watched Josh walk slowly toward the other side of the playground, dragging a stick across the chain link fence as he went. He approached a group of Grade 5 boys at play. Laura had overheard him talking to a couple of them one day in the library. The three of them had been deep in conversation, comparing the merits of books on dinosaurs. Josh joined their informal game of soccer, then at the sound of the bell, walked happily back to the building with his "library buddies," chatting all the way. This was a different child from the one she'd observed only a few minutes ago.

Jennifer Todd, on the other hand, had spent her recess very involved in playing house with a small group of girls from Laura's class. Jennifer adjusted very well to school. She was, in all respects, the model student—well behaved, careful, and attentive. Her academic skills were exactly as expected for the beginning of Grade 1. Laura didn't know quite what to make of the note the principal left in her box this morning, but she began to connect its contents with the folder the Todds had left for her on the first day of school.

Well, maybe it was time to have a closer look at that folder's contents and at the report Josh's mother brought in. Mrs. Cameron was adamant that the psychologist's assessment be considered in planning Josh's program, but Laura had put her off, saying she preferred to get to know Josh better herself first. She had told the Todds the same thing. Laura stuck the note from her principal, the folder, and the report in her briefcase next to the set of reading evaluations she had collected from her beginning readers before organizing her class for the rest of the morning.

That evening ....

Nathan Golden, Ph.D.
Clinical Psychologist

1125 Doncaster Road

Fort Woodward, Ontario

555-9877

August 10, 1998

Mr. and Mrs. Edward Cameron brought their son, Joshua (BD July 3, 1992), for an intellectual and academic assessment on August 3 and 6, 1998. Joshua will begin Grade One in September of this year at his neighbourhood school. Mr. and Mrs. Cameron had questions about Joshua's school adjustment. They are considering whether Joshua should skip Grade One. They requested an assessment to gain information on the level of his abilities and academic skills in order to help them make informed decisions about his education. They also expressed concern about his social development, noting that he had a difficult time making friends in kindergarten. In addition, they noted that he has problems relating to neighbourhood children. He invites them to play but his ideas for play often seem too complex for them.

Joshua's parents provided the following background information. Mr. Cameron was accelerated in school, and entered university early where he completed a master's degree in engineering. Mrs. Cameron began university with her age group. After completing her B.A., she proceeded to earn a Ph.D. in linguistics. Joshua's parents strive to provide an enriched environment for him and model a love of learning. Joshua is Mr. and Mrs. Cameron's only child.

Joshua developed a love for reading at the age of four and a half, and he reads everything he can. By five and a half, he was reading children's novels. Joshua is inquisitive about a wide range of subjects but his passion is dinosaurs. His parents reported that he has many models and engages in elaborate play with them. He has read many books about dinosaurs and knows the subject in depth. His parents were not aware of just how much he knew until they took him on a summer trip to Drumheller's dinosaur park.

I administered a standardized intelligence test on August 3 and two academic achievement tests on August 6. In addition, Mrs. Cameron completed a social skills rating on her son. On both testing occasions, Joshua presented as a well-behaved and very intelligent child. He conversed with ease about the books he read this summer and his trip to the dinosaur park. He was keen to take part in all test activities and worked diligently.

On the Wechsler Intelligence Test for Children—Third Edition (WISC—III), a test of general cognitive ability, Joshua scored at the 99th percentile overall. This level of performance is attained by only one percent of children of Joshua's age. Joshua demonstrated very superior performance across all subtests of the verbal and performance scales.

To test academic achievement, I administered the Kaufman Test of Educational Achievement (K-TEA) and the General Information subtest of the Peabody Individual Achievement Test—Revised (Piat-R). Joshua's scores on the K-TEA were as follows:

Reading decoding	91st percentile
Reading comprehension	93rd percentile
Spelling	75th percentile
Mathematics computation	94th percentile
Mathematics application	99.6th percentile

On the Piat-R General Information subtest, Joshua scored at the 96th percentile.

Mrs. Cameron rated Joshua's overall social skills as average. This overall rating includes average self-control, above average cooperation, and fewer than average assertive behaviours, including initiating social interactions and responding to others' actions. Mrs. Cameron also perceived that Joshua demonstrates fewer than average responsible behaviours, mainly in areas that require initiating social contact. Joshua demonstrates fewer than average behaviour problems (including internalizing, externalizing, and hyperactive behaviours).

Joshua demonstrated a number of exceptional strengths in this assessment. His reasoning abilities and his academic achievement are outstanding. In both assessment sessions, Joshua was engaged and highly motivated to solve the problems presented to him. It was clear that he loves learning and responds well to challenges. He certainly would benefit from an educational program that is appropriately matched to his level of ability and that challenges him and extends his thinking.

Mrs. Cameron's concerns about Joshua's social development are supported by her ratings of his social skills. In his relationships with age peers, Joshua was seen as ill at ease and lacking in confidence. Joshua needs the opportunity to work with students of similar abilities in order to share and develop his interests and expertise.

N. Golden

Nathan Golden, Ph.D.
Registered Psychologist

FORT WOODWARD ELEMENTARY SCHOOL

Memo: Principal's Office

To: Laura
From: Ken
Date: Sept. 24, 1998
cc: Jennifer Todd

Laura, I thought you'd be interested in the attached. It was in this morning's paper. Mrs. Todd called me late yesterday afternoon to tell me it would appear today. She's very concerned that Jennifer's not being challenged and that her behaviour at home has changed since she started school. Could we talk about this after the staff meeting Thursday afternoon? Thanks, Laura.

Fort Woodward Sentinel

September 24, 1998

Editorials

As parents of a young daughter who has just started school, we are gravely concerned about the school system's inability to provide programming that is sufficiently challenging for their brightest students. In the few short weeks since school began, we have watched our daughter change from an energetic and inquisitive youngster who soaked up knowledge like a sponge to a passive recipient of the most fundamental of academic skills. We're not speaking out against the teaching of basic skills; rather, we object to their teaching to children who mastered them long before they entered school.

If our brightest children aren't sufficiently challenged by their academic programs from the first moments they enter school, what's the lesson they learn about the value placed on knowledge and the inquiring mind? We fear that this most important of school experiences may leave a lasting unfavourable impression. Our hope is that by speaking out in a public way at this early stage of our child's development, we can somehow effect change.

Elaine and Jack Todd

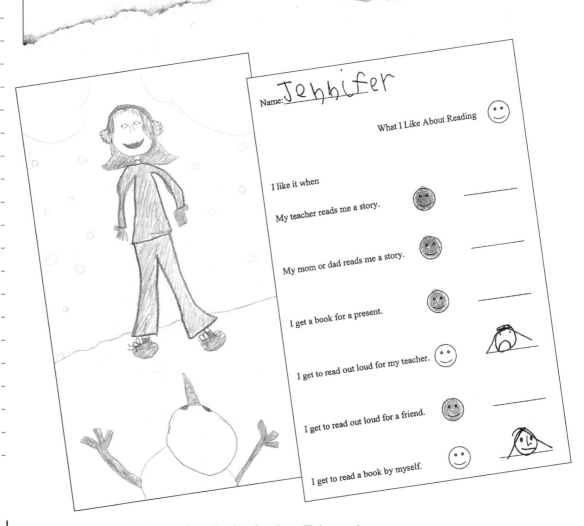

THE TODDS

Elaine, Jack, and Jennifer

August 28, 1998

Dear Ms. Webster,

Since we're new to Fort Woodward Elementary, this letter is to introduce our daughter Jennifer to you. As she is about to begin Grade I, we wanted you to know some of her developmental milestones.

Jennifer talked very early—at about 9 months old. Ever since then we've been astounded by the growth of her vocabulary and the sophistication of her verbal abilities. She's very interested in language, and loves to know where words "come from" and to explore their meaning in depth. She started to read at three—and now reads short children's novels, often one or two a week. Going to the library is one of her favourite pastimes.

Jennifer taught herself keyboarding in kindergarten. She loves to write stories on the computer. She's also a poet, but prefers to have us record her poems. She chose the story and the poem in the folder especially for you. She also chose the drawing from some she did last winter.

It is our hope that Jennifer's first experience at Fort Woodward Elementary will encourage her to delight in the challenge of learning. We'd be pleased to meet with you at your convenience to discuss Jennifer's education.

Sincerely,

Elaine and Jack Todd

One day there was a little girl who wanted to find out if there was really a pot of gold at the end of the rainbow. She REALLY wanted to have a pot of gold. She dreamed she could be a BIG QUEEN one day and rule the whole world. She really liked that thought. So every day she would go out into the forest where she lived. When she would see a rainbow she would always look for the end of it.

One day as she was looking for it, her mother called, "Your lunch time's ready." She rushed toward her mother and said, "Mommy, can you put my lunch in a little bag? I want to find the gold at the end of the rainbow." Well her mother was a very kind woman so she packed her a lunch and said, "Be off with you." And then she scurried off. It had been raining a fair bit and the sun was shining while it was raining so she looked and there was the rainbow. She followed it and suddenly she found a big cave full of gold.

Little did she know there was a snake hungrily waiting for her. She really wanted it so she jumped in. Because she had been so happy she threw her apple down in the gold and it hit the snake's head. And the snake gave up on her. It died and she was rich. Then her and her mother lived happily ever after.

By Jennifer Todd, age 5

Fire Poem

Fiery breath of the dragon.
Its yawn makes the colours of the autumn leaves.

Jennifer Todd, age 5 $\frac{1}{2}$

File 3

Adam

Fran Briscombe gazed thoughtfully at her Grade 3 students as they began to work, with varying degrees of concentration, on their Math seatwork. It was the second week in October, time for IEP conferences to begin, and with this in mind she searched out Adam Mathieson. What would she have to say at Adam's IEP conference?

Adam, eight years old, had what the audiologist termed a "moderate to severe high frequency sensorineural hearing loss bilaterally." As far as Fran was concerned, this meant that Adam was hard of hearing in both ears and that he had some difficulty pronouncing certain sounds (for example, he tended to substitute *s* for *sh,* so that *shoulder* became *soulder* and *leash* became *leass*). Adam wore a hearing aid on each ear, and Fran used an FM system, which resembled a portable transistor radio, to help Adam hear her class instruction. With the help of twice-weekly visits from the hearing resource teacher and the half-time presence of a special education assistant, Adam was progressing well in all areas, with the possible exception of reading comprehension and following verbal directions, which remained problematic areas for him. But Adam was a quiet, pleasant boy who worked diligently in class and enjoyed making friends, and Fran was pleased to have him in her class.

No, Fran's main concern for Adam did not pertain to his academic performance. She was more troubled by the social difficulties he seemed to be experiencing on the playground recently. One of the more aggressive boys in the class had been teasing Adam about his hearing aids, and just this morning at recess his verbal taunts had escalated to pushing. Fran had intervened, but she was disturbed by Adam's inability (or unwillingness?) to deal with his aggressor. Moreover, for the past week Adam had refused to wear his hearing aids for most of the day, and Fran knew that without them he could follow little of the verbal instruction or discussion in class.

Prior to the IEP meetings in the school district, each IEP participant was asked to complete a student information form. The compiled forms were then sent to each participant before the meeting in order to provide everyone with a well-rounded view of the child. Fran had just received the compiled report on Adam this morning. Perhaps it would give her some ideas of how to help Adam—and herself—cope constructively and assertively with the bullying.

SUMMARY FORM—STUDENT INFORMATION PROFILE

(Composite of Student Information Profile Forms completed by IEP participants two weeks prior to the IEP meeting)

Completed forms submitted by: Bill and Sue Mathieson (parents), Fran Briscombe (classroom teacher), Catherine Edgars (vice-principal and teacher), Judy Schwartz (special education assistant), Eleanor Green (hearing resource teacher)

The following information is provided in order to help set goals for Adam's Grade 3 year:

1. Adam's strengths:
   - likes school—is keen
   - wants to read—is showing more motivation to read than last year
   - more easygoing than in previous years
   - cooperative
   - socially—is doing better, especially in 1:1 situations
   - good sense of humour
   - keeping up in Math
   - will ask for help when encountering difficulty with seatwork

2. Adam's weaknesses:
   - getting information and following directions that are based on auditory skills
   - social skills—following cues of others
   - difficulties in understanding rules in games, at times
   - expressive language difficulties (word retrieval)
   - dealing with bullying

3. Some of Adam's interests:
   - reading
   - playing the piano
   - going to Scouts
   - hiking/biking
   - playing with action figures
   - making friends

4. Some hopes/dreams/goals for Adam:
   - that Adam maintain his confidence
   - that he continue to enjoy reading
   - that he learn to be more assertive in his communication skills
   - that he learn repair strategies to help him communicate more effectively
   - that he continue to become more independent and confident

5. Some concerns/fears/nightmares that we might have for Adam:
   - that there would continue to be a lack of understanding in some social situations
   - that he would not continue to enjoy school
   - that he withdraw socially because of inabilty to cope with teasing and bullying

File 4

Yetta

Dianne Collie was stumped. In her 15 years of teaching she had worked with students with a variety of special needs—learning disabilities, cerebral palsy, visual impairments, Down Syndrome. When she learned two months ago, at the end of August, that a profoundly deaf student, Yetta Clarke, was to transfer from the Provincial School for the Deaf into *her* homeroom, she thought she'd have no difficulty learning about and accommodating the unique challenges to this student's learning. She had even been excited at the prospect of learning American Sign Language!

However, American Sign Language (ASL) had not proved so easy to learn, and with all the demands on her time during September, Dianne had been grateful for the easy access to communication with Yetta that Jasmine, the educational interpreter, provided. In fact, Dianne thought guiltily, she had relied on Jasmine too much, allowing her to have more contact than Dianne had with the Hearing Resource teacher and even agreeing for her to adapt the language level in the texts when necessary. Now, at the end of October, it was apparent that Yetta had settled well socially into the integrated experience, and so it was time, Dianne thought, to focus more directly on Yetta's academic performance. It was here that Dianne was baffled.

When Dianne spoke with Yetta (through Jasmine) yesterday and suggested that she focus on improving her English grammar, Yetta had been resistant—even defiant. Her hands were clearly expressing anger when she signed that she could learn only through ASL, and that English grammar was important only to hearing people. Yetta accused Dianne of neither appreciating nor understanding ASL and Deaf culture. Deaf culture? What on earth did *that* mean? And what was the difference between ASL and English? Dianne didn't know the answers to these questions, but she realized that in order to be an effective teacher for Yetta she needed to find out. . . .

North Ashland School Board
INDIVIDUALIZED EDUCATION PLAN

Date: _October 1999_

Name (last /first):

Clarke , Yetta

Birthdate: _84/04/22_   Age: _15_   Sex: _F_

School: _Ashland Secondary_

Home Address:

237 Parkhurst Drive

North Ashland

Grade or Program: _10_

Classroom Teacher: _Dianne Collie_

Parent / Guardian:

Carol & Mark Clarke

Hearing Res. Teacher: _Joanne Embleton_

Transportation: _n/a_

Parent / Guardian Phone #:

_635-2114_

Emergency Phone #:

639-8212 (Dad's work)

Parent Signature: _Carol Clarke_

First Language: _English / ASL_

School History: _For Preschool Yetta attended the Mt. Seymour Deaf Children's Development Centre. She has attended the Provincial School for the Deaf since kindergarten._

Siblings / Ages: Social Factors: Group/Foster Home & Phone #:

Calvin   13yr.   —   —

Social Worker & Phone #:

—

Medical Alert/Conditions:

Yetta has a profound bilateral sensorineural hearing loss which she acquired at the age of 3½ due to meningitis.

Support Services & Specialized Equipment:

Yetta receives full-time support services from the educational interpreter, as well as direct services from the Hearing Resource Teacher and the Skills Development Teacher.

Ashland Secondary School

INDIVIDUAL EDUCATION PLAN

CONFIDENTIAL

This Individual Education Plan (IEP) is designed as a working document to give teachers an overview of the student's strengths and weaknesses. It also includes a checklist of recommended adaptations and strategies to use when working with this particular student.

Student: Yetta Clarke   **Date:** October 1999

Strengths:

- pleasant, cooperative, good sense of humour
- works well with her interpreter
- wants to do well
- very social, well adjusted
- good student
- loves sports and other extra-curricular activities

Weaknesses:

- has a profound hearing loss
- sometimes is a bit too social
- has difficulty with Math
- could work harder on her studies

Additional Comments:

Yetta has had a good start to this school year. She has developed good friendships, which is especially important because this is her first term integrated into a regular public school. We are now working on having her realize when she can visit and when she must work.

It's very important for Sarah Fox, Yetta's interpreter, to be informed as soon as possible as to what topics, concepts, and vocabulary will be covered next in Yetta's classes, so that Sarah can be prepared (for example, learn the exact spelling of new vocabulary words).

Yetta receives additional assistance from Joanne Embleton, the Hearing Resource Teacher, three times a week.

Please let me know if you have any concerns about Yetta.

David Anson, Skill Development Teacher

RECOMMENDED ADAPTATIONS AND STRATEGIES

Adaptations Required: Instructional (circle those applicable)

- Reduced Assignments
- (•) Taped Novels/Textbooks
- Summaries (from the Resource Room)
- Calculator
- (•) Peer Note-taking   *interpreter will copy*
- (•) Photocopy of Overheads
- Highlighted Texts (from the Resource Room)
- Alternative Texts
- Other

Assessment (circle those applicable)

- Adapted Tests/Exams
- Allowing extra time
- Testing done or finished in the Resource Room
- Exams done or finished in the Resource Room
- Reader (a trained Special Ed. Dept. staff person)
- Scribe (a trained Special Ed. Dept. staff person)
- Dictaphone/Tape recorder
- Other

Additional Strategies (circle those applicable)

- (•) Provide written back-up for oral directions.
- See that homework is in a written form and copied down by the student.
- Ask the student to repeat directions to you.
- Pair the student with a "good" student (the "buddy" system) to check on homework assignments being copied down, notes correctly copied.
- Seat the student close to the teacher.
- N/A • Avoid student oral reading.
- Give course outline and lists of vocabulary to the Skill Development (SKD) teacher.
- Give a copy of test or assignment to the SKD teacher so that the student can be "primed."
- Allow students to use vocabulary cards or note cards.
- Allow reasonable time extension for assignments, if appropriate.
- Do not penalize for spelling errors.
- Send assignments to the SKD teacher if they need editing or re-copying.
- Break long-term tasks into small units—with corresponding due dates.

Recommended Reporting Procedure (circle appropriate choice)

- (•) Adaptations only   Provincially approved letter grade
- Significant modifications   Modified letter grade (as needed)

File 5

Brian

As the rain beat relentlessly against the tall windows of his classroom, Jeff Davis took a moment to watch his Grade 9 students at work on a set of Math problems. It was a rare quiet moment in the class; perhaps the rain was setting a pensive mood. This class was an unusual mix. About a third of the students more or less successfully struggled to keep on top of the work; another third seemed indifferent, more concerned with life at the mall than with school; and most of the rest handled the work well. Then there was Brian. Jeff was so used to dealing with comic books and *Playboy* magazines underneath textbooks that he hadn't known what to make of finding a calculus text concealed on Brian's desk. He hadn't reacted, but had any of the other kids noticed? Brian already seemed to be apart from this group. How would they react to this?

Brian slowly got up and approached Jeff, a puzzled look on his face. He quietly asked a challenging question about algebra and appeared satisfied with Jeff's response. It was obvious that Brian thought about mathematics more deeply and certainly at a higher level than the other kids in the class. Jeff felt uneasy. He was already challenged by Brian's questions and bothered by the fact that Brian earned very high marks that seemed an imperfect reflection of his ability. What should he do about this, if anything?

On the one hand, Jeff was excited by Brian's eager mind. Brian had an amazing thirst for knowledge. On the other hand, Jeff doubted his own ability to challenge Brian and felt unsure if he should even try in the context of this class. Brian's mother was pretty vocal about Brian being moved into a Grade 12 Math class, but the school was resistant to the idea and Jeff worried about such a placement. He had skipped a grade in elementary school himself and had felt like an outsider all through high school—too young to have a driver's licence and too young to date.

Well, maybe it was time to have a closer look at the report Brian's mother brought in awhile ago. Jeff had skimmed it then but hardly knew what to make of what he saw. At the time, it had only made him feel more inadequate to meet Brian's needs. Now he stuck the report in his briefcase before organizing the class with their homework assignment. He'd better have another look.

That evening . . . .

JENNIFER SHORT, Ph.D.

Clinical Psychologist
146 Elm Lane
Littleton, Alberta
555-0032

CONFIDENTIAL REPORT
PSYCHOEDUCATIONAL ASSESSMENT

DATE:	September 10, 1998
NAME:	Williams, Brian
BIRTHDATE:	July 3, 1984
AGE:	14 years 2 months
GRADE:	9
PARENT(S):	Mr. and Mrs. Edward Williams
ADDRESS:	634 Maple Street, Littleton, AB
HOME PHONE:	555-8791
ASSESSMENT DATES:	August 31 and September 2, 1998

BACKGROUND

Brian, a 14-year, 2-month-old boy, is currently enrolled in Grade 9 in a public high school. According to Brian, he's "bored" in the public school environment. He reported that he'd like to be able to do more challenging work, particularly in Math. He feels he's "marking time" in class.

Brian appears to have a good relationship with his family. He has one older sister, age 16. Brian reported that he gets along very well with her. Brian has a group of two or three friends with whom he spends time out of school. He reported that he has nothing in common with his schoolmates.

Brian is concerned that he's small for his age and would like to be bigger. Mrs. Williams indicated that Brian was often sick in his early childhood. Despite these early concerns about his health, Brian has an otherwise normal developmental history.

In terms of academically related skills, Mrs. Williams reported that Brian has some specific strengths and interests. Brian is very curious, especially about how things work. He's also a fast learner, able to work well independently when interested in a subject area. Brian enjoys reading and is most interested in science fiction. He's also highly interested in mathematics and shared his wish to pursue mathematics at university. Brian reportedly has great determination and a high level of concentration. Generally, Brian is doing well in school.

Mrs. Williams is concerned about Brian's self-confidence. Brian is very compliant and Mrs. Williams feels this may impact his progress at school. She's particularly concerned with determining his overall ability and his academic strengths in order to help her advocate for his education and to help him to gain a better sense of himself as a capable student. Mrs. Williams also expressed some concern about Brian's social relationships at school.

Stanford-Binet Test of Intelligence—Fourth Edition (SB-4)

This is a test of general cognitive ability in which children's performance over a broad variety of tasks is compared with the performance of other children their age. The SB-4, like other IQ tests, measures only a portion of the competencies involved in human intelligence. The results of IQ tests are best seen as predicting current performance in school, and reflecting the degree to which children have mastered the middle class symbols and values. This is useful, but it's also limited. IQ tests don't measure innate-genetic capacity and scores aren't fixed. Some persons do exhibit significant increases or decreases in the measured IQ.

Child performance on the SB-4 is interpreted in terms of a Total Test Composite, Verbal Reasoning, Abstract/Visual Reasoning, Quantitative Reasoning, and Short-Term Memory scores. The Total Test Composite is a summary IQ score reflecting overall test performance and is usually considered to be the best measure of cognitive ability, general intelligence, scholastic aptitude, and readiness to master a school curriculum. Children's Total Test Composite IQ may be affected by their motivation, interests, cultural opportunities, natural endowment, neurological integrity, attention span, ability to process verbal information (particularly on the verbal subtests), ability to process visual information (particularly on the performance subtests), and conditions under which testing occurs. The Verbal Reasoning score is a measure of verbal comprehension, which includes the application of verbal skills and information to the solution of new problems, ability to process verbal information, and ability to think with words. The Abstract/Visual Reasoning score is a measure of perceptual organization, which includes the ability to think in visual images and to manipulate these visual images with fluency and relative speed, to reason without the use of words (in some cases), and to interpret visual material quickly. The Quantitative Reasoning score measures knowledge of mathematical operations, mathematical applications, and flexibility with numbers and mathematical symbols. The Short-Term Memory score is a measure of meaningful and random units of stimuli presented either visually or verbally.

Educational Implications

Verbal Reasoning. The verbal reasoning scale provides information about a child's ability to process and reason with language, and to attend to language-based problems.

Abstract/Visual Reasoning. The abstract/visual reasoning scale provides information about a child's ability to process visual-spatial material, to plan and organize, to attend to problems that involve visual-spatial material, and to learn and remember nonverbal information. Spatial abilities are important in mathematics, science, and the arts.

Quantitative Reasoning. The quantitative reasoning scale provides information about a child's ability to process numerical information, to apply mathematical knowledge to practical applications, and to plan and organize quantitative material.

Short-Term Memory. The short-term memory scale provides information about a child's ability to learn and remember both visual and verbal material. Short-term memory has direct implications for following directions in academic settings.

Total Test Composite. The total test composite provides information about a child's general intellectual ability, aptitude to learn, and ability to achieve in school. There is a strong relationship between Total Test Composite IQ and school achievement.

On the SB-4, the average range for general scores is 89–110.

	GENERAL SCORE	SCORE INTERVAL	CLASSIFICATION	*PERCENTILE
Verbal Reasoning	143	137 - 150	99.64	Very Superior
Abstract/Visual Reasoning	147	141 - 153	99.83	Very Superior
Quantitative Reasoning 1	61	155 - 166	>99.97	Very Superior
Short-Term Memory	128	122 - 134	96	Superior
Total Test Composite	154	149- 159	99.96	Very Superior

* A percentile score indicates that the examinee's score is equivalent to or superior to the given percentage of the population of individuals of that age.

The chances that the range of scores described in the intervals above includes his true IQ are about 95 out of 100.

Observations of Performance

Brian's overall performance as indicated by the Total Test IQ score falls into the very superior range. This level of performance is attained by less than 1% of the population.

Brian demonstrated superior performance across all the domains of the SB-4. His greatest strength appeared to be in the quantitative reasoning domain. Performance on this set of mathematical tasks may be influenced by the degree of experience with similar tasks, but also indicates exceptional development of Brian's mathematical abilities. The results of this intellectual assessment appear to be valid.

Woodcock-Johnson Psycho-Educational Battery—Revised (WJ-R): Tests of Achievement—Standard Battery

This is a recently revised (1989) battery of individually administered academic achievement tests that measure various aspects of scholastic achievement in basic academic skills, reading, mathematics, and written language, and general knowledge in the area of Sciences, Social Studies, and Humanities. Test items on this measure do not necessarily measure achievement within any specific school curriculum, but rather reflect more general academic achievement and development of skills across the assessed domains. Individual performance on the battery of achievement tests is interpreted in terms of each of five achievement cluster scores. The Broad Reading score reflects ability to identify letters and words, and use of vocabulary and comprehension skills. This is a broad measure of reading achievement, including performance of both oral reading and passage comprehension tasks. The Broad Mathematics score reflects performance in mathematical calculation, and the analysis and solution of practical mathematical problems. The Broad Written Language score indicates achievement in written language achievement including both single-word responses and production of written responses to pictorial and written cues. This cluster score reflects achievement in the application of skills in spelling, punctuation, capitalization, and word usage, as well as overall quality of expression in written form. The Broad Knowledge cluster score provides a measure of the extent to which the child has achieved a general knowledge of concepts and vocabulary in various areas of sciences, social studies, and art, music, and literature. The Skills cluster score is an index of general achievement in prerequisite academic skills, including language and mathematics performance. Achievement cluster scores in the range of 90–110 are representative of average performance. Percentile scores for each academic cluster are also reported. Percentile scores can provide a means to compare the child's performance with the performance of other children of the same age who have completed this battery. A percentile score represents the percentage of the population who achieved at the same or lower level of performance on this cluster of academic skills. For example, a percentile score of 95 for a cluster indicates that the child's performance is most like the top 5% of children of the same age who completed this cluster in the battery of tests. This would be a superior level of performance in this area of academic achievement.

The following table presents the results of the current administration of the WJ-R Standard Achievement Battery:

ACHIEVEMENT CLUSTER	SCORE	PERCENTILE
Broad Reading	138	99
Broad Mathematics	168	99.9
Broad Written Language	137	99
Broad Knowledge	125	95
Skills	144	99.8

Brian's performance on this battery of academic achievement tests was at the very superior classification level. As on the SB-4, Brian has exceptional ability across all areas of academic achievement, with his highest results in the area of mathematics. The percentile score of 99.9 in Broad Mathematics indicates very superior performance, an achievement level equal to or better than that attained by 99.9 percent of children his age. Brian's "lowest" score appears to be in the Broad Knowledge domain, but still equals or exceeds the performance of 95% of his same-age peers.

Social Skills Rating System

The Social Skills Rating System provides a measure of student social behaviours that can influence the development of social competence and adaptive functioning at school and at home. Scores from the rating forms are combined to produce ratings of social skills, academic competence, and problem behaviours as perceived by the student, the parent, and/or the teacher. Standard scores with a mean of 100 and an average range of 85 to 115 are reported here along with a "confidence band" that indicates the range of scores that would be expected 95 percent of the time. A percentile rank is also reported. This is the percentage of individuals in the student's age group who would achieve the same score or a score lower than the student. Subscale ratings, which group behaviours as occurring more, average, or fewer times than age peers, are also reported.

Brian and his mother completed ratings. Overall, Mrs. Williams rated Brian's social skills as average (standard score of 98; confidence band 91 to 105; percentile rank 45). Brian is seen as demonstrating average self-control and above-average cooperation. He is believed to demonstrate fewer than average assertive behaviours, including initiating social interactions and responding to others' actions. Brian was rated as demonstrating fewer than average responsible behaviours, mainly in areas that require initiating social contact. Brian rated his own social skills as average overall (standard score of 106; confidence band 94 to 118; percentile rank 66). Brian rated cooperation, assertion, self-control, and empathy all as average.

Overall, Brian demonstrates fewer than average problem behaviours (standard score of 81; confidence band 77 to 85; percentile rank 10).

SUMMARY AND RECOMMENDATIONS

Brian demonstrated a number of exceptional strengths in this assessment. His reasoning abilities and his academic achievement are outstanding, particularly in mathematics. In both assessment sessions, Brian was engaged and highly motivated to solve the problems presented to him. It was clear that he loves learning and responds well to challenges. He would certainly benefit from an educational program that is appropriately matched to his level of ability and that challenges him and extends his thinking.

Mrs. Williams' concerns about Brian's social development are supported by her ratings of his social skills. In his relationships with age peers Brian was seen as ill at ease and lacking in confidence. Brian himself rated his social skills as average.

Brian needs the opportunity to work with students of similar abilities in order to share and develop his interests and expertise.

It was a pleasure to work with Brian. If I can be of any further help in addressing questions, please don't hesitate to contact me.

Jennifer Short

Jennifer Short, Ph.D.
Registered Psychologist

File 6

Allan and Melanie

As Fran Simons, the Director of Special Education, left the room Margaret tried to figure out how she was going to organize her kindergarten classroom this year. Fran's visit had been scheduled for the week before school began so that they could go over some data collected by a doctoral student last year. For his thesis on cognition and school readiness he'd tested pre-schoolers in several rural communities. In the parental permission for this testing it was stipulated that the information would be made available to the Director of Special Education to be used for screening purposes. Fran and Margaret had worked closely in the past trying to identify as early as possible those students who needed extra attention or help. But this year they had some advance information on several students, which would make it possible to plan activities before school began.

Now Margaret needed to sit down with the material to analyze it in detail. Overall, her class was a pretty average mix of boys and girls from a variety of backgrounds. The school had a nice ethnic mix, ranging from new European and Asian immigrants to First Nations students. The two files Margaret was particularly interested in required some analysis and thoughtful planning.

Melanie had had a rough start in life. Even though the chemotherapy was successfully over there were still the social and emotional problems to deal with. And Allan, one of five First Nations students, would be a delightful challenge. Margaret was the kind of teacher who prided herself on being prepared to provide the individual attention she felt these children needed as they started school.

Memorandum

TO: *Margaret Dembrowski*
FROM: *Fran Simons, Director of Special Education*
RE: *Confidential Test Results*

Here are photocopies of the summary test results we discussed on the phone. The tests include:

Peabody Picture Vocabulary Test—Revised (PPVT)
*Bracken Basic Concept Scale—School Readiness Composite and
    Full Scale*
Kaufman Assessment Battery for Children (KABC)
Expressive Vocabulary
Gestalt Closure and Hand Movements
Revised Brigance Diagnostic Inventory of Early Development

I think we covered most of the details, but if you have any further questions please give me a call.

EARLY CHILDHOOD ASSESSMENT

CONFIDENTIAL

Name: _Melanie McKay_

Community: _A-4_

Birth Date: _1/22/93_

Date of Assessment: _4/18/98_

Age at Assessment: _5 years 4 months_

	Raw Score	Standard Score	Age Equivalent			
1. Peabody Picture Vocabulary (Receptive)	37	83	3	Yr	9	Mo
2. Bracken Basic Concept Scales (Receptive)						
a. Color	10 /10					
b. Letter Identification	6 /10					
c. Numbers, Counting	4 /14					
d. Comparsions	0 /7					
e. Shape	2 /20					
* School Readiness Composite (SRC)	22	6	3	Yr	10	Mo
f. Direction/Position	24	8	3	Yr	10	Mo
g. Social/Emotional	11	6	3	Yr	4	Mo
h. Size	10	10	4	Yr	10	Mo
i. Texture/Material	7	7	3	Yr	2	Mo
j. Quantity	10	5	3	Yr	0	Mo
k. Time/Sequence	6	6	3	Yr	0	Mo
* Total Score	84	67	3	Yr	6	Mo

	Raw Score	Standard Score	Age Equivalent			
3. KABC Processing Scales						
a. Face Recognition						
(Simultaneous)	12	12	6	Yr	6	Mo
b. Gestalt Closure						
(Simultaneous)	10	9	5	Yr	0	Mo
c. Hand Movements (Sequential)	9	11	6	Yr	0	Mo
d. Number Recall (Sequential)	10	13	8	Yr	3	Mo
4. KABC Expressive Vocabulary	14	80	3	Yr	9	Mo

	Age Equivalent		
5. Brigance			
a. B6 Hopping	5	Yr 5	Mo
b. B9 Catching	4	Yr 5	Mo
c. B11 Ball Bouncing	4	Yr 8	Mo
d. C2 Block Tower Building (# of Blocks=12)	5	Yr 5	Mo
e. C5 Draw A Person	5	Yr 4	Mo
f. C6 Forms Coping	5	Yr 9	Mo
g. C7 Cutting With Scissors	5	Yr 2	Mo
h. Body Parts Receptive (English)	4	Yr 0	Mo
i. Visual Discrimination			
Two Symbols	5	Yr 9	Mo
Three Symbols	5	Yr 9	Mo
j. Recites Alphabet (Letters correct=25)	5	Yr 2	Mo
k. Counting (Highest number=19)	5	Yr 9	Mo

EARLY CHILDHOOD ASSESSMENT

CONFIDENTIAL

Name: _Allan Duncan_

Community: _A-4_

Birth Date: _10/1/93_

Date of Assessment: _8/15/98_

Age at Assessment: _4 years 10 months_

	Raw Score	Standard Score	Age Equivalent			
1. Peabody Picture Vocabulary (Receptive)	50	91	4	Yr	6	Mo
2. Bracken Basic Concept Scales (Receptive)						
a. Color	10 /10					
b. Letter Identification	10 /10					
c. Numbers, Counting	14 /14					
d. Comparsions	4 /7					
e. Shape	14 /20					
* School Readiness Composite (SRC)	51	10	5	Yr	4	Mo
f. Direction/Position	54	14	7	Yr	2	Mo
g. Social/Emotional	28	15	6	Yr	10	Mo
h. Size	15	15	7	Yr	10	Mo
i. Texture/Material	13	8	4	Yr	10	Mo
j. Quantity	32	12	6	Yr	0	Mo
k. Time/Sequence	31	13	6	Yr	2	Mo
* Total Score	224	112	6	Yr	2	Mo

	Raw Score	Standard Score	Age Equivalent		
3. KABC Processing Scales					
a. Face Recognition (Simultaneous)	12	12	6	Yr 3	Mo
b. Gestalt Closure (Simultaneous)	15	14	7	Yr 3	Mo
c. Hand Movements (Sequential)	9	12	6	Yr 0	Mo
d. Number Recall (Sequential)	7	10	5	Yr 0	Mo
4. KABC Expressive Vocabulary	19	107	6	Yr 3	Mo

	Age Equivalent		
5. Brigance			
a. B6 Hopping	5	Yr 5	Mo
b. B9 Catching	5	Yr 0	Mo
c. B11 Ball Bouncing	4	Yr 8	Mo
d. C2 Block Tower Building (# of Blocks=12)	4	Yr 1	Mo
e. C5 Draw A Person	5	Yr 0	Mo
f. C6 Forms Copying	6	Yr 5	Mo
g. C7 Cutting With Scissors	5	Yr 0	Mo
h. Body Parts Receptive (English)	5	Yr 0	Mo
i. Visual Discrimination			
Two Symbols	5	Yr 10	Mo
Three Symbols	5	Yr 10	Mo
j. Recites Alphabet (Letters correct=25)	5	Yr 2	Mo
k. Counting (Highest number=21)	5	Yr 8	Mo

File 7

Joey and Monique

It was 3:30 on a stormy November afternoon. Donna Tremblay needed some breathing space and time to think, so she retreated to the staff room and poured herself a mug of coffee. Donna was particularly concerned about two children in her Grade 3 class—Joey and Monique. Each had experienced a particularly difficult day.

First Joey. Reflecting on the day, Donna realized that most of the activities she had planned involved some written work, not Joey's strong point. He usually did almost anything to avoid it—talking (preferably to her about his latest invention), taking an exceptionally long time to get organized, or "spacing out." Today was a day when, in addition to *all* those strategies, he got involved in a fight with another child—not his usual pattern, but it did happen from time to time. Nobody seemed to know how it got started. What a contrast to his "success stories"! Donna thought about his enthusiasm and commitment to the school science fair.

When Joey was involved in science projects he was focused and cooperative. Donna also noticed that he tried to write more if science was the focus of the writing assignment—but with a lot of difficulty. She really should have let him tape-record some work today. His taped stories were always better than his written ones.

Strange, though—he could really handle felt pens and paint brushes. Along with his knowledge of science, Joey's claim to fame among his classmates was his amazing artwork.

In a lot of ways, Monique was just the opposite of Joey. Her artwork was quite immature. Today Donna tried to help her organize a title page for science. Monique's first attempt was two tiny stick figures and a sun in one corner of the page. After Donna showed her the covers of some books and drew an example of how a title and a picture can be organized on a page, Monique crumpled up her new attempt, put her head down on her desk, and cried. Then there was gym.

Donna had six stations organized in the gym. The children "numbered off" so they knew where to start. Monique should have started at Station Four but somehow got confused. The other children teased her, calling her "dummy." Donna got that straightened out but soon heard Monique scream in frustration. Donna could hear the children at her station calling, "NO, Monique! You're supposed to start *behind* the red line. *Pay attention.*" What was up? Did she really not get it?

Donna felt as if she'd been torn in different directions all day. She needed some guidance about how to help Joey and Monique as soon as possible.

I Just finished space acadamy and Im
going on a trip to mars. I can see shooting
stars, planets and other space ships to. when I
reach mars I emiedeatly start diging. I reach
3 feet when I hit something.

by Joey

Joey's prehistoric story (tape recorded October 17, 1998)

Once there was this guy and, um, he was this old guy and he was
really wise. And he told—he kept on telling everybody that there
was a beast—that there were beasts that were coming to the land.
And that they were going to charge everybody and stomp on them
and crush them and kill everybody. But nobody believed him. So the
guy knew that it was going to happen, so rather than just waste his
time telling the people that this monster was coming 'cause he knew
that—'cause they weren't believing him, he just went up to the
mountain . . . um . . . to save his own life. So he climbed up the
mountain and found a magic jewel and it said on it, "He who holds
this jewel will defeat anyone—can defeat anyone." So he thought,
"Hmm, maybe I can use this to defeat the beasts and save our
land." So—but he didn't see the small print that said, "But—um—the
beast—but . . . ."

And it said, "But if the beasts find the jewel, they will take it." But
he didn't see the its . . . the printing. So he put it down. He climbed
down the mountain, went back to his village, and he said, "Hey
everybody, I've got the magic jewel that can kill the beasts!" But
nobody . . . still nobody believed him. And the next morning the
beasts came and everybody was scared frozen. And nobody could
do anything because they were so scared. So—ah—so the guy
threw—thought—thought that if he threw the jewel at the beast
then it would go into his stomach and kill it and kill the beasts. But
when he threw the jewels, it didn't do anything. Instead, the beast
ate the jewels and the jewels were lost forever. And so—um, the
people—um, well, the people were all killed and . . . the beasts ate
themselves all up. So everyone was dead. The end.

Lynnwood Elementary

Math assessment: Review of addition skills

Name: Monique   Date: Sept. 10/98

Basic facts to 10: Oral recall	Couldn't do in her head or by using the number line.
Basic facts to 20: Oral recall	Not done.

$$\begin{array}{c} 2 \\ +8 \\ \hline 10 \end{array} \qquad \begin{array}{c} 5 \\ +4 \\ \hline 9 \end{array} \qquad \begin{array}{c} 7 \\ +1 \\ \hline 8 \end{array} \qquad \begin{array}{c} 4 \\ +1 \\ \hline 2 \end{array}$$

$$6 + 3 = 1 \qquad 3 + 7 = 5 \qquad 2 + 5 = 8$$

File 8

Amy

Dianne Takahashi had taught Social Studies and English at Maplewood Secondary School for four years. With only a short time left before summer she had stayed late for a meeting at the request of Chris Graves, the Vice-Principal. He'd contacted all the teachers who'd be getting Amy in their class next year. The counsellor felt it was important to start September off right with Amy, especially since there was the transition into a secondary school. Everyone had met Amy when she came to visit the school along with the other Grade 7 classes. Dianne had worked with several special needs students in her regular class, but this was her first experience with a student who had Down Syndrome. Dianne had read articles in *Readers Digest* and had a little background knowledge from old Biology classes, but she didn't really know how to approach planning for the school-based team meeting. Since this student was being included in all of the regular Grade 8 classes it meant the team meeting would consist of about ten people.

The hardest part was that Dianne knew she'd need to be totally prepared with goals, objectives, and strategies if she were to participate. With such a large group Chris wouldn't have much patience with an unprepared teacher. This school prided itself on the inclusiveness of its classes and the support that teachers gave to students with special needs. With all this in mind Dianne started to work through the folder, knowing she'd need to figure out how to accommodate and modify her plans so that Amy could participate in the Grade 8 Social Studies class. The counsellor had even included a copy of the form that would be filled out indicating her plans for Amy in Socials 8.

IEP FOR AMY SMYTHE

The following suggestions have been made by Greg Black, the counsellor working at Evelyn Park Elementary School.

Amy should begin Grade 8 in as many regular classroom situations as possible. While there may be specific goals for her in the IEP the overall plan should be to provide her with vocational and life skills to give her as much independence as possible. Teachers should plan goals and objectives with this in mind. In Grade 10 she should begin a Work Experience Program. Emphasis for academic skills should include:

1. Reading. Examples: directions, understanding signs.
2. Mathematics. Examples: money, time, measures, consumer buying.
3. Social Studies. Examples: general government organization, taxes.
4. Art. Examples: risk-taking, non-verbal expression.
5. P.E. Examples: healthy living, active community participation.
6. Computers. Examples: programs to enhance reading, etc.

Both the Grade 6 and Grade 7 teachers agree that Amy is more capable than the formal test results indicate. This is also supported by Dawn, the teaching assistant. Amy has tremendous support at home. Both older sisters work with her to develop different life skills. Teachers need to understand that Amy is a very willing participant in the classroom, sometimes to the point where she may disrupt lessons. There is a need for patience and assisting Amy to understand behaviour appropriate to a situation.

When Amy is angry or hurt she'll sit in a corner of a room (sometimes she'll cry) until she works it out for herself. These episodes are becoming more infrequent as she matures and develops alternative coping strategies. She's often teased by other students, but doesn't always understand what's happening.

Amy is a hesitant reader at approximately the Grade 2/3 level of understanding. Her math is at about the same level. Teachers at the elementary school have found Amy resistant to using materials that are different from those of other students. While the secondary teachers may use specialized materials, they may find that modifications of regular materials work as well.

PARENT

SURNAME: _Smythe_

MOTHER: _Marilyn_   FATHER: _Walter_

MOTHER'S WORK PHONE: _555-9826_ FATHER'S WORK PHONE: _555-3619_

STUDENT FULL NAME: _Amy Ruth Smythe_ D.O.B. _03/11/86_
                                                    D/M/Y

STUDENT PREFERRED NAME: _Amy_ PHONE NUMBER: _555-4129_

1. The best thing school has provided my child is _friendships_
and social skills.

2. My child has struggled with _academics - especially_
reading and math.

3. In high school my child could use some help with _reading and_
math for everyday living

4. I anticipate my child's high school life to be _fun. She enjoys school_
and being with people her own age.

5. My child's strengths are _1) a very willing worker 2) gets_
along well with others 3) likes to try new things

6. My child's interests and hobbies outside school are _being "water girl" for her_
sisters soccer teams. Playing Barbie with
her sisters.

7. My feelings about High School are _We are both fearful since_
this is the beginning of her becoming an adult.
What will happen to her when we are no
longer able to care for her? Can she have
some independance? Will she improve
her reading and life skills beyond where
she is now? Will she be a burden on
her sisters lives in the future?

STUDENT

ELEMENTARY SCHOOL NAME: _____ YEAR: _____

STUDENT FULL NAME: _Amy Smythe_____ D.O.B._____
_____ D/M/Y

ADDRESS: _____

STUDENT PREFERRED NAME: _____ PHONE NUMBER: _____

* Language spoken most often at home: _____

* In grade 8 I would benefit from the following: (please circle the ones you think you will need)

    (YES / NO) - Resource Room   (YES / NO) - Learning Assistance
    (YES / NO) - Counselling   (YES / NO) - An elective instead
                                          of French.

1. Right now I think school is _____fun_____

2. Going to high school will be _____scary_____

3. I learn best when _____Dawn Helps me_____

4. One subject in school that I have a hard time with is _____Math_____

5. One subject in school that I find easy is _____art_____

6. One thing I like about myself is _____my eyes and my hair____

7. My family is _____nice_____

8. My attendance at school is _____good_____

9. One thing that worries me is _____being laufe at_____

10. When I am angry or frustrated I _____cry_____

Student Background

Name: Amy Smythe

Age: 14yrs. 2mo.

Address: 112 Fort Lyone Road., Maplewood

Phone: 555-4129

Mother's Name   Marilyn Smythe

Address
(if different from above)

Work: p/t 555-9826   Home: 555-4129

Father's Name   Walter Smythe

Address
(if different from above)

Work: 555-3619   Home:555-4129

Legal Guardian   Walter and Marilyn Smythe

Work: Home:

Family Information: Amy lives with her parents and 2 older
sisters. Mr. Smythe Works as a truck driver
for Harrison Cartage while Mrs. Smythe is a
part-time secretary in a dentist office.

School	Year	Grade	Placement
Evelyn Park Elementary	1989	Passing	Regular Class-
			Pull-out program

MEDICAL HISTORY

Medical History: <u>Amy is a child with Down Syndrome. Amy had surgery for a heart valve problem when she was a toddler. She has no other major health problems. During the spring Amy has hay fever attacks which are controlled by antihistamines. She is in very good health. There are no constraints on her activities.</u>

Medications: NONE.

Formal Assessments

Type P.P.V.T. - R	Evaluator Mathew Allen	Date 04/94
Result C.A. : 10yrs. 6mo.		
S.S. 81		
%ile 10		

Type WISC – 3ʳᵈ. ED. Grade 6	Evaluator Mathew Allen	Date 01/96
Result	Freedom from Distract SS 74	Verbal IQ 79
Verbal Comprehension SS 81	Processing Speed SS 69	Performance IQ 66
Perceptual Organization SS 71		Full Scale IQ 78

Type Vineland Adaptive Behaviour Scales	Evaluator Resource Class Teacher Mary Chilldon	Date 11/96
Result Communication 68	Adaptive Beh. Composite 71	
Daily Living 72		
Socialization 85		

Informal Assessment

Observation:
Amy loves sports, but has some skill problems. The other students generally work around this issue.

Setting: P.E.

Focus: Interaction and skill level.

Date: Oct. 1997

Observation:
Amy is a happy young lady. She is a very willing worker — likes books. She does rely on Dawn (the TA) quite a bit. However, with help she can accomplish more than was expected. Other students come to her assistance as well even when not asked. Keeps on task.

Setting: Regular classroom — Grade 6.

Focus: Attitude and academic skills

Date: Dec. 1997

Observation:
Amy can function in the cafeteria with a minimal amount of supervision.

Setting: Lunch room

Focus: social interaction and skills necessary to eat lunch (with clean up)

Date: Sept. 1997

Goals

Goal:
Current Level of Performance:
Class:

Objectives	Evaluation

File 9

Trevor

It was Kathy Lee's first official day at her new elementary school. She'd spent the last two weeks moving her materials into the portable classroom that would house her Grade 4 class. She then arranged displays and learning centres and planned for the new term. Now, before her pupils arrived, she just had time for a trip over to the main school to get some library books. Then all would be ready for her new students.

Bob Sawchuk, the librarian, was friendly and helpful. He was also sympathetic as he said, "Oh. *You* have Trevor this year."

"What do you mean?" asked Kathy. She felt both disturbed and apprehensive.

"Well," continued Bob, "he was here a year ago and caused no end of trouble. He threatened his teacher with a knife a few times, bullied other kids, and stole anything that wasn't nailed down. Last year he was at another school, but now he's back. I think there's been some kind of custody battle. Poor kid. But he sure can disrupt a school."

Kathy carried the books she'd chosen back to her classroom, feeling considerably more tentative than she had just a short while ago.

Half an hour later Trevor arrived at the portable door with his grandmother, who greeted Kathy pleasantly and said, "Trevor's living with me now." Trevor was polite and settled down to the "Getting to Know You" activities planned for the morning. Soon the noises started, vague little grunts and bits of songs. The other children complained, and Kathy asked Trevor to stop. "Okay," he said, and did stop for a while. Otherwise the day went fairly smoothly, though Kathy did notice how much difficulty Trevor had writing a few sentences. It was Trevor's drawing of his favourite activity that really upset her, though. Clearly she'd need to know more in order to help him. After school, she went to the office and requested Trevor's confidential file. Then she got a cup of coffee from the staff room and went back to her desk in the portable.

SEPT 21, 1998

Dear Miss Lee,
I think you should know that Trevor is living with me because his father couldn't take care him. He beat him alot. His mother took off when Trevor was a baby. Trevor will stay with me and his granddad now. We're getting custody. Let me know if theres any trouble at school.

Lina Hall

Kathy Lee   6:37 PM   10/02/98   questions

Date: Fri, 2 Oct 1998   18:37:13
Subject: Questions
To: Danielle Langer <danielle.langer@sdK.portferris.ca>
From: <kathy.lee@sdK.portferris.ca> (Kathy Lee)

Dear Danielle,
I'm new at Port Ferris Elementary this year. I have Trevor Hall in my class. I know it's only the beginning of the year but I'm really worried about him. What really scares me are his drawings. He draws knives dripping with blood all over his work and men hanging from gallows on the covers of all his books.

I just had a look through his confidential file again and I have a lot of questions. Would it be possible for us to meet soon and talk over my concerns?

Thanks very much, Danielle.

Kathy

Date: Tues, 13 Oct 1998 08:45:06
Subject: Meeting
To: Kathy Lee <kathy.lee@sdK.portferris.ca>
From: <danielle.langer@sdK.portferris.ca> (Danielle Langer)

Dear Kathy,

I'd be happy to meet with you. I assessed Trevor two years ago. I'm very busy right now with the assessments for the new program at the secondary school and won't have any time available until late November. Could we meet after school, say 4:00, on November 26 at my office.

Danielle

Danielle Langer, M.A.
School Psychologist
Port Ferris School District

NOV 14, 1998

Dear, Miss Lee
    I have your note about Trevor needing new exercise books. I bought him 6 new ones a month ago! Whats going on? I cant afford all these school supplys.

Lina Hall

File 10

Chris

As Anne filled out the report on Chris she tried to understand the complexity of what Chris's parents had gone through before they arrived at their decision. Up until this year Chris had been an average to good student academically. He was on the rugby team and was well-liked by students and teachers. He had expressed an interest in Forestry as a career, following in his father's footsteps. Anne understood from the counsellor that his elementary school years had been filled with problems. He'd been in constant trouble with teachers and had done very badly in his academics. It had been hard to imagine this delightful, intelligent young man was the same anxiety-filled person the counsellor was talking about. That is, until this year. Grade 11 was such an important year— a time when students needed to pull it all together if they were to go further with their education—and yet it was all falling apart.

Anne had had Chris in her Grade 8 English class, so she thought she knew what to expect, but so far this year had been very difficult. Chris had been diagnosed as ADHD in Grade 7, when his parents had decided to start him on medication. It seemed to work very well, and over the years Chris became more organized and focused on his schoolwork. This past summer Chris had been in for his yearly physical when the doctor noticed some changes in his liver function. Even though his parents were aware of the small chance of this side effect of Cylert, the medication Chris was taking, they panicked. Chris was taken off all medication. Now some of the issues, which had been the reasons for the medication in the first place, had resurfaced.

Anne was faced with the report requested by the parents and counsellor. There would probably be a school-based team meeting, which would embarrass Chris and cause him further problems with his friends. Not only that, but she had to figure out how to work with Chris to get him back on track academically. If he were to go to university for Forestry there had to be some major changes in English.

December 7, 1998
RE: Christopher Vance
Grade 11 English, Block C

During the past term I've had an opportunity to observe Chris in a variety of classroom situations. Since I had Chris in Grade 8 English I can compare his conduct and work then and now. At your request I've used the two sample observation forms you gave me in order to try to be as precise as possible in my observations. Listed below is a summary of these observations.

1. Chris often has trouble getting started on seatwork. He'll look around the room and find excuses to leave his seat, e.g., sharpening a pencil, borrowing paper, making comments to his neighbours.

2. Other students in the class find these interruptions annoying, so there's usually some kind of discussion or comments, which in turn interferes with everyone getting down to work. I think this is having some adverse effects on his friendships, judging by the comments I've overheard.

3. Chris has difficulty remembering sets of instructions. He'll often turn in work that's incomplete and not realize what's wrong. The lists of instructions I give him are often left somewhere or lost completely.

4. Chris turns in papers with mistakes that I know he shouldn't be making.

5. I've seen a great deal of frustration in the past few months. Chris becomes angry when papers are returned with comments and grades that are much lower than he expects. He's even started to use the "I don't know" phrase in class, even when I know he has the correct answer.

6. His best time of day is when C block is first period of the day. His worst time is at the end of the day when he becomes more disruptive (asking inappropriate questions) and failing to complete in-class tasks (even group work).

I'm very concerned about Chris. He's intelligent and, up until recently, hard working. I find it frustrating to see this change in his behaviour and academics. Please keep me informed about any decisions made.

Sincerely,

Anne

File 11

Paula

Marilyn watched the girls line up to start the shooting drill. They were all pretty serious about making the girls' basketball team. While all of the Grade 8s and Grade 9s were placed on a team, everyone knew that by Grade 10 they had to really shine in order to be selected. Marilyn knew that for many of them being chosen for the team meant automatic acceptance into the social circle at the high school. Since basketball was such a popular sport both the boys and girls teams became a big social draw during the long dark days in this northern mining community. The regional high school drew students from several outlying communities, so for many the size and layout of the building was daunting.

Of particular interest to Marilyn was a slight girl named Paula. Paula was a talented player who excelled in basketball in elementary school. The counsellor had asked Marilyn to observe Paula in her P.E. class as well as at practice, because Paula's parents had been concerned about a steady loss of weight since last January. The family doctor had been keeping track of the situation and found her to be completely healthy, except for being underweight. The parents hoped that joining a team sport might encourage an increase in appetite, as well as ease the transition to high school.

Marilyn had been chosen for this informal observation because she'd been instrumental in introducing the "Moving to Inclusion" program to the district's physical education teachers. The counsellor had given Marilyn the usual set of general information that the Grade 7 teachers prepare about their students to introduce the high school teachers to the incoming Grade 8s. Marilyn wanted to review that sheet, as well as add a few more notes to her half-written report to pass along to the counsellor. She'd been watching Paula for about five weeks now and was becoming more concerned about what she was seeing. Throughout all of this Marilyn wondered how she was going to work with Paula over the coming year.

STUDENT INTRODUCTION FORM

Student: Paula Osmund

Grade 7 Teacher: Richard McArthur

I'm delighted to introduce Paula Osmund to her high school teachers. This is a student who's been a terrific kid to have in class. She's a friendly, cooperative, and conscientious student. Her academic work is good to excellent, although she often speaks in such a soft voice that it's difficult to understand what's being said. Paula has been on the basketball, baseball, and gymnastics teams during elementary school. I know she wants to be on the girls high school basketball team like her sister was two years ago.

Paula has always been a popular student. She was elected president of the Grade 7 class this year and took this responsibility more seriously than any other Grade 7 I've taught. She has a small group of girlfriends whom she associates with during school. I understand they socialize together outside of school as well.

I'm aware of some concern by her parents regarding a loss of weight since Christmas. I understand there is no medical problem. The only time I've noticed any change in Paula is during free time, when she often sits alone with a blank look, as if her thoughts are somewhere else. And when she receives a paper back she perceives any comments as negative criticism and becomes very quiet. Since Paula has had a series of colds that she can't seem to get rid of I'm assuming this is the reason for her change. By the end of the summer she'll have had a chance to rest up, so I'm confident that her start in high school will be great.

October 13, 1998

Dear Brian,

At your request I am forwarding this written report on my informal observations these past two weeks of Paula Osmund, Grade 8. I've had opportunities to interact with her in my Block C girls' P.E. class as well as during girls' basketball practice. These observations have included out-of-class times as well, such as in the hallway and cafeteria. While I've been assured that there are no medical problems, I'd like to voice my concern over Paula's weight. At first I thought it might be part of the normal adjustments that adolescents undergo during puberty, however on closer observation I'm no longer convinced this is the issue. I've listed below a summary of these observations. I know you're meeting with the parents, and I hope this will help them and the doctor to assess Paula's condition.

Please let me know the outcome of your meeting. If we're to be of any help to Paula we'll need to approach this issue together.

Yours,

Marilyn

1. Paula is an excellent student. She's attentive and works very hard to make any work turned in as perfect as possible. She was handing in a paper when she noticed a misspelled word. She refused to hand it in but spent her break time re-copying it, even though I assured her it was all right.

2. While she's an avid basketball player she has problems with stamina and strength exercises. Her attitude, skills, and team awareness are good to excellent. She's overly hard on herself if she misses a play, often frowning and chewing on her lower lip. I know she jogs and exercises to a video every day.

3. In the cafeteria and after practice, when the other girls are snacking, Paula will eat a carrot stick. On one occasion I made a point of watching this group of girls. While the others passed around chips, chocolate bars, and granola bars Paula bypassed all of it to eat a total of one, cut carrot stick. She told the others that she wasn't really hungry because she'd eaten a big lunch and didn't want to get fat. Since I'd been on cafeteria duty that day I knew she'd eaten only a couple of pieces of lettuce and a bite of an apple. I'd seen her give away her lunch to a girl who'd forgotten to bring a sandwich that day.

4. Paula is very conscious of her appearance. Even during a practice she'll keep a hairbrush in her bag to use while sitting at the bench. When I commented on it she responded that she always wanted to look her best.

File 12

Peter

On an early November afternoon after his students left for the day, Mr. O'Shea (called "Mr. O" by his Grade 6 class) began to review his notes and his students' portfolios. He planned to make a start on writing comments for report cards, but he also felt that there were a few students about whom he needed to think more extensively. One of those students was Peter. Peter appeared to have resisted all Mr. O'Shea's efforts to foster a sense of community and self-esteem in his class. Thinking about the few times when Peter seemed engaged and part of the class, Mr. O'Shea puzzled over the lack of a consistent pattern in what might account for that engagement. Mr. O'Shea found it really hard to get a good read on Peter's capabilities.

Peter had been a student in Elm Grove Elementary since kindergarten. Mr. O'Shea reviewed Peter's permanent record and copies of his previous report cards in October and was very surprised to find that, up to the end of Grade 4, Peter's academic progress was above average and no behavioural or social concerns were mentioned. In Grade 6, though, he seemed to be a different kid. He appeared unmotivated; assignments were rarely completed, and when they were they were done halfheartedly. Peter spent a good deal of class time drawing or telling jokes to classmates. In cooperative learning situations Peter's participation was minimal. The other kids enjoyed his jokes, but there was an increasing reluctance to have Peter join groups. "He just goofs off" was the usual complaint. Peter's claim to fame in the classroom was his drawing ability, but even this wasn't helping him to gain acceptance.

According to Peter's previous teacher, his lack of motivation started at the beginning of Grade 5. Peter's parents expressed concern at that time; they too seemed puzzled by the change. They requested regular updates on his progress and expressed willingness to help in any way they could. A homework book was started, which helped to keep Peter on track for about a month. His parents tried rewarding "good days" at school and at home, and a new bike was promised if an A was earned on his last report card in Grade 5. These attempts didn't produce any lasting change in effort or behaviour.

Mr. O'Shea felt that his attempts to get the MacDonalds involved this year weren't going anywhere. He called Peter's mother to arrange an appointment to talk over Peter's progress. During that call he offered to talk about things they might try together to help Peter's motivation. Mrs. MacDonald said that she and her husband were really running out of patience. They'd tried everything last year and they thought it was his job to straighten things out. Mrs. Macdonald put off making an appointment, saying that she'd check with her husband first.

Mr. O'Shea found it difficult to get to know Peter. The reading log gave a few clues but Peter revealed little about himself. In September, the class was asked to write five sentences about themselves, describe their most important strength, and tell about something they'd like to improve. They also drew self-portraits. Their self-descriptions and self-portraits were included in their portfolios. Mr. O'Shea looked at both of these efforts now. Peter's description of himself was completed at home because he hadn't finished it in class. Mr. O'Shea remembered Peter showing it to him proudly despite it still being incomplete; he'd done it on his new computer.

What to do next? This was the big question. . . .

I am a complicated person. I don't like to talk about myself.

My most important strength is that I have a rich fantasy life.

It's hard to improve on . . . PERFECTION.

Problem-Based Learning in Inclusive Education

Books I Read In __September/October__

Name __Peter__   Mark chapter books with a *.

Fiction				Non-Fiction			
Date started	Date finished	Title	Author	Date started	Date finished	Title	Author
Sept 2	Sept 7	Redwall *	unknown	Sept 11	Oct 11	Reptites Mag.	Various
Sept 9	Sept 21	Redwall *	unknown	Oct 11		" "	"
Sept 22	Oct. 1	Dracula *	Bram Stoker				
Oct. 2	Oct. 24	Rapter Red *	unknown	Sept. 29	Oct 3	Sports car International	"
				Oct. 14	Oct 15	Mountain bike action Mag.	"

Ministry of Education

Student Record Card—Page 2

Family Name: <u>MACDONALD</u>

Given Names (first, middle): <u>PETER SCOTT</u>

Birth Date (D/M/Y): <u>02/12/87</u>

Achievement Record

(Average grade for year)

Subject	YEAR: 96–97 GRADE 4	YEAR: 97–98 GRADE 5	YEAR: 98–99 GRADE 6	YEAR: GRADE	YEAR: GRADE
Language Arts	A	C+			
Mathematics	A	C			
Science	A	C-			
Social Studies	B	D			
Physical Education	B	D			
Fine Arts	A	B			
French	B	C-			

File 13

Jason

Arnie Williams had been a secondary Science teacher for eight years now. It always amazed him how September seemingly disappeared into a haze of papers, kids, and the usual cold which he got each year at this time. As he always said to his wife (who got the cold too), "There's nothing like watching Grade 9s use their homework papers to cover a cough before they hand it in." His teaching load this year consisted of two Grade 9 Science; two Grade 11 Biology, and one Grade 12 Biology. What this meant was that it was almost mid-October before he had enough grades and was sufficiently organized to really scan his grade book. That's when Jason's name showed up.

Jason Reynolds sat at the back right corner of the classroom. His interest, attention, and lab work in Science class were average (along with the average amount of whispering, girl watching, and note passing). He hung out with a group of identically dressed boys and considered lunch and hallways the best part of school. In other words, he was a typical Grade 9 boy. What caused his name to show up were his grades. While homework had been handed in, it was usually incomplete or poorly done. The lab grade was 60%; weekly quiz average so far was 44.75%; the first unit test averaged 49%; and now the unit test from Friday averaged 41%. The lab grade was the easiest to explain, since they worked in groups and helped each other out with the experiment and answers. But none of the quizzes or tests had been that difficult. There was a discrepancy between what Arnie saw Jason doing in class and the grades he was getting.

After the last-period class on Tuesday Mr. Williams asked Jason to stay for a couple of minutes to talk about his grades. Jason was a nice kid, and as he explained to Mr. Williams, the grades were very easy to understand—he had a learning disability and he couldn't learn Science. Since the school was very conscientious about notifying all teachers of any special needs students this information took Arnie by surprise. It took a bit of questioning, but finally it came down to an elementary teacher who'd told Jason and his parents that his problem in school was a learning disability. Jason had been pleased because it finally got his parents off his back.

It took Arnie almost a week before he got an answer from the counselling department. Now he knew he had to make some decisions about what he was going to do with Jason in Science.

Name: Reynolds, Jason
Student Number: 806977
Class: SC 9B
Date: October 10, 1998

Weekly Quiz

#1   44%
#2   52%
#3   35%
#4   48%

AV. 44.75% (Class Average=72.3%)

Unit Tests

Chap. 1-3   49%
Chap. 4-5   41%

AV. 45%   (Class Average = 67.1%)

Assignments

Lab. 1-1   60%
Lab. 2-2   65%
Lab. 2-6   56%
Lab. 3-1   62%
Lab. 5-2   55%

AV. 59.6% (Class Average = 75.2%)

Homework

p. 23   12/20
p. 31   3/10
p. 45   9/20
WKST 1   6/10
p. 54   INCOMPLETE
WKST 2   INCOMPLETE
WKST 3   INCOMPLETE

MEMO FROM COUNSELLING

To: *Arnie Williams*
From: *Mary Asche*
Date: *Oct. 22, 1998*
RE: *Jason Reynolds*

I've finally been able to get through to Jason's parents to follow up on your inquiry. They confirmed what Jason said. The Grade 4 teacher explained to them that Jason was having some problems reading and this was "often" (their words) a sign of LD. Since that time they've been satisfied if he just passes.

There are no other records beyond the permanent record which shows quite a few barely passing grades. (Actually, they seem to be getting worse each year.) Standardized screening tests give no indication of any problems. There are no social or emotional problems mentioned.

If you think it should be pursued further please work on the enclosed form for the school-based team meeting in four weeks. I'll add the permanent record, etc. before the meeting. Be very specific, since we're overloaded as usual.

JERRYS COVE SECONDARY SCHOOL BASED TEAM

Must be received by the chairperson at least two days prior to scheduled meetings

Student Name:_____ Date: _____

Counsellor:_____ Estimated Time Needed: _____

Identify the concern and interventions attempted by student and staff:

_____

_____

_____

_____

( ) Student schedule attached
( ) Current grades / progress indicated on schedule
( ) Attendance records attached

Comments (include any parental/guardian contact):

_____
_____
_____
_____
_____
_____
_____

Review Date:_____

File 14

Françoise

Helen took a few moments while the class was working quietly to observe Françoise in the front row. This class had been fairly difficult to organize into that cohesive, cooperative grouping Helen enjoyed teaching. But now it seemed they were finally starting to understand how the groups were supposed to collaborate, and her Constructivist teaching style was beginning to pay dividends—with one exception.

Françoise had retinitis pigmentosa, a progressive degeneration of the retina. According to the counsellor and school nurse, Françoise would probably become totally blind by the time she entered adulthood. It was hard to believe that this overly quiet girl with no apparent friends in school would have so many other difficulties in her future. Even when working in her group Françoise would answer only direct questions, and respond with monosyllables to any attempts by the other girls to chat, effectively shutting down any attempts at communication. At the moment she could read with difficulty, but at least she was still coping with the work in Grade 10 Social Studies. Modifications had been made so that many things were in larger fonts when necessary (thanks to the computer), and Helen often taped readings and classes. Also, she was always very careful about decreased lighting in the room.

What bothered Helen the most was the note waiting in her box this morning from the counsellor. The big challenge now was how to include Françoise fully into all the class activities. Then came the question of what would happen to her socially and career-wise in the future. Helen knew she had to do something about this.

November 3, 1998

Dear Helen,

I finally got through to the parents of Françoise Tan. While Françoise was born here in Canada, her parents are Vietnamese. They don't speak English very well, so I had to rely on a visiting neighbour to interpret for us. Apparently they feel the field trip is not appropriate for Françoise and that she should be spending her time in the Resource Room working on her reading. I know you have a series of field trips planned for class projects, but the Tans are very protective of Françoise and don't see the value of field trips for her. Apparently the Vision Specialist has had the same response to the issue of learning Braille, so you're not alone. Perhaps you could arrange for another assignment while she works in the Resource Room.

Harry

File 15

Lily

"Tonight's the night," Linda Weston told herself, "I've got to get started on report cards or I'll never be finished on time." She organized coffee, pupil files, and her computer and sat down to work. The kitchen table would look like this for the next week at least. The first two reports were straightforward. Then Linda reached for Lily's file. Lily Drexall—where to start?

Lily was one of the ten Grade 3s in Linda's multi-age classroom of Grades 3, 4, and 5. She was achieving at the mid-Grade 1 level in Math, and had pre-reading skills and emergent writing skills. Lily's intellectual disability became evident when she started kindergarten, and at the end of that year the district's school psychologist had assessed her. She scored 65 on an IQ test and was found to have significant problems with adaptive behaviour. Linda reviewed the assessment and thought how familiar the observations were—difficulty staying on task, memory and reasoning problems, delayed language development and social skills, poor gross and fine motor skills. An IEP had been in place since Lily began Grade 1, and was reviewed by the school-based team at least twice every year. Linda continued to monitor Lily's IEP and look for innovative ways to modify her academic program and make her social skills development effective.

Lily's classmates tried to be understanding and helpful, but her inattention and disruptive behaviour sometimes made them resentful. Lily was often excluded from recess and lunchtime activities and the children resisted her inclusion in cooperative learning activities. As challenging as all this was, Linda felt that she had a good handle on how to help Lily. Progress, while slow, was evident. It was communicating the reality of Lily's challenges to her parents that caused Linda some concern. Foremost in her mind was the conversation she'd had with Mr. and Mrs. Drexall on "Meet the Teacher" night. Mrs. Drexall opened with "What's all this talking and playing around stuff Lily's doing?" Linda had answered carefully, "We're doing some activities that should help Lily get along better in the classroom. If she learns how to work better with other children, it should help her learning. She'll be able to concentrate on her schoolwork more." Mr. Drexall responded, "Well, forget all that stuff. You teach her to read better and everything will be dandy. We want her to go to university and earn lots of money so that she can take care of us for a change." Linda thought about that conversation, together with the memo from the school-based team coordinator. Communication about Lily's needs was going to be difficult. The blank screen seemed to stare back at Linda.

Memo:

To: Linda
From: Stu
Date: November 3, 1998

Hi Linda. I know it's early in the year, but I've been thinking we should get a meeting of the team together to review what we're doing for Lily. Her transition to Grade 4 is going to need some thought. You're doing such a wonderful job of supporting her developmental needs. Maybe you have some thoughts about what should happen in the intermediate grades, and how we can smooth the way. Let me know a good time for you to meet. Thanks!

Ministry of Education

Primary Grades Progress Report—Fall Term

Student's Name: Lily Drexall

School: Pacific Elementary School   Date: November 9, 1998

In the primary grades, the following goals are emphasized:

Intellectual development, social development and responsibility, emotional development, physical development, and artistic development. These goals are met through an integrated approach to curriculum.

Comments:

_____   _____
Linda Weston, Teacher   Joan Chen, Principal

File 16

Susie

It was November, time for the first report cards to be done. Tanya Green had set aside some evenings to work on the reports and felt satisfied with her progress so far. But then she reminded herself that there were some challenges ahead, both in writing helpful reports to parents and in her own planning for several children in her class. She decided to focus on Susie next—little Susie who seemed to have so many things to cope with at eight years old. Susie appeared to enjoy school, and took an active part in Tanya's multi-age classroom of Grades 1, 2, and 3 pupils despite her academic difficulties.

Susie could read material at the mid-Grade 1 level. Her progress has been very slow, despite the learning assistance she'd received since she started school. Tanya had an individualized reading program in place, so Susie's reading curriculum was appropriately matched to her ability. Susie's written language skills were weak too, but she tried valiantly to keep up with other children her age. Her Math skills, on the other hand, were solid. She reasoned and computed with ease.

Susie was a very kind, helpful child. Her comments in class discussions showed sensitivity to others and maturity in thinking of ways to solve classroom issues. Younger children often turned to her for help. Tanya reflected that she, too, often felt somehow reassured after talking to Susie.

But Susie frequently arrived at school looking very pale and tired. She had numerous responsibilities at home as the eldest of three children, and often talked about babysitting her younger brother and sister. Susie's mother would drop in occasionally to bring Susie's lunch or homework. Her visits were pleasant but short, and she too looked very tired. Tanya had wanted to meet with her, but she hadn't returned the letter from the school asking parents to indicate the most convenient time for them to attend an open house and student-led conference.

Tanya looked back and forth at the drawing Susie had presented to her that morning and the "Who am I?" entry in Susie's portfolio, and wondered how and where to start. Maybe filling out an IEP form would help. At least it would get her started on detailing Susie's strengths and learning needs and thinking about how to address both. And doing that would help her with report card comments.

Individualized Education Plan

Student Name: _____

Date of Birth: _____

School: _____

Grade/Teacher: _____

Parent/Guardian: _____

Phone: _____

Abilities and Interests	*Learning Needs*

Learning Goals and Objectives

Curriculum Area:

Current Level of Achievement:

Objectives	*Strategies/Resources*	*Evaluation*

Learning Goals and Objectives

Curriculum Area:

Current Level of Achievement:

Objectives	*Strategies/Resources*	*Evaluation*

Learning Goals and Objectives

Curriculum Area:

Current Level of Achievement:

Objectives	Strategies/Resources	Evaluation

Who Am I?
I am a girl. I am 8.
I like to ride a Bike.

I Like to iceskate.

File 17

Ruth

Bill watched as his last class of the day filed out of the room. It had been one of those days—again. After five months of teaching Ruth in Math class, and all the meetings he'd had, he was hoping that this time things might be different.

Ruth had gone into a *grand mal* seizure just as the class was beginning to work on their practice exercises. Over the past few months the medication had helped reduce these more dramatic events. The class was exceptionally good about these occurrences, and knew what to do without even being told. One designated student went to the office for the nurse, while the rest picked up their materials and quietly walked to the library to finish their work. Maybe it was the efficiency of the routine that bothered Bill the most. Last year in Grade 8 Ruth had been a bright, gregarious teenager with a passion for multi-coloured nail polish. Now she was a reticent, introverted teen with very low self-esteem. The idiopathic epilepsy had appeared without any warning just as the summer was beginning. While most of the time the seizures were *petit mals,* resulting in a confused look, they were also often accompanied by drooling, which bothered Ruth more than her headaches did. Her friends were trying to be supportive, but Ruth was so embarrassed that she was alienating herself from them. Bill figured it didn't help to have a father who treated the whole problem as if she had a mental illness that brought disgrace to the family. The counsellor had told Bill all this when he inquired about observing her eating alone at lunch.

As Bill looked over his Seizure Observation Form for the doctor and school office he knew he needed to figure out a way to work with Ruth that would both enhance her self-esteem and get her to work with groups in class.

SEIZURE OBSERVATION FORM

Student's Name __Ruth Cutter__

Teacher's Name __Bill McCarty__

Date of Seizure __Jan 14, 1999__

Time of Seizure __0920__

Duration of Seizure __Ca. 2 min__

*

Classroom Activity Prior to Seizure:

I had just finished an explanation using the overhead. The class was working on 3 practice problems. I was walking around helping students.

Behaviour Prior to Seizure:

Ruth didn't start working right away, but seemed to be daydreaming. She said "Oh, no", seemed to pass out and slid to the floor.

Behaviour During Seizure:

Ruth caught her breath, then started to thrash. After a short time she seemed to be asleep. The sleep only lasted a brief time.

Behaviour After Seizure:

Ruth was confused and had a headache. She started to cry when she realized what had happened and complained of a headache.

Teacher Response and Comments:

As explained in previous reports, the class has a procedure which they follow in the event of Ruth's having a seizure. I moved desks away and held her head to one side because she was drooling. I tried to reassure her everyone understands and generally tried to calm her down.   * Nurse arrived ca. 0925

File 18

Su Ling

Dave Lamont finally left school at 9:00 p.m. He'd stayed late that evening to see several students and their parents for their first student-led conference of the year. Dave ventured out into a storm—fitting night, he thought, after the way the conference with Su Ling and her parents had gone. Dave was angry with himself. He could have handled the conference so much better.

The Tangs had immigrated to Canada from China two years ago. Dave knew they were working very hard to establish themselves. Su Ling was their oldest child; she had a brother in Grade 1 and a three-year-old sister. Her little brother was very bright, and Dave knew his teacher was having a hard time giving him enough challenges. At the last school-based team meeting there had been some discussion of accelerating him.

Su Ling, on the other hand, was struggling in a number of curricular areas. From her first day in his Grade 5 classroom Dave had been trying to figure out how best to teach her. Su Ling's English was poor, despite having received ESL support for two years, and it was affecting her achievement in Language Arts, Social Studies, and Science. She did really well in Math, except when she had to read problems; her artwork was great, and she did well in gym. She was also well accepted by the other children.

In preparing her portfolio for the conference Dave had helped Su Ling focus on Math and Art. He'd also let her choose some photos of a field trip to show her parents. There were some great shots of Su Ling and her friends panning for gold. After putting her portfolio together they had rehearsed some things she could tell her parents.

Everything had gone well at the conference until Dave introduced his concerns about Su Ling's English. The Tangs were clearly upset by their daughter's lack of progress. They both spoke fluent English and told Dave that both English and Cantonese were spoken at home. But when Dave introduced the idea of a home–school plan to help Su Ling they had appeared very hesitant. Dave felt he had made a grave error in presenting his concerns to the Tangs, but he wasn't sure just where he'd gone wrong. Was it the concerns themselves, or the way he'd presented them?

Dave resolved that tomorrow he would talk to Jane, who worked twice a week with Su Ling on English acquisition, and get her perspective. He and Jane had talked about seeing the Tangs together some time after the student-led conference. Jane had thought it might be helpful to have Su Ling assessed. Dave wondered how the Tangs would feel about that.

```
Jane Grunwald      4:15 PM    11/03/98              referral
```

Date: Tues, 3 Nov 1998 16:15:23
Subject: Referral
To: Dave Lamont <dave.lamont@sd80.langton.ca>
From: <jane.grunwald@sd80.langton.ca> (Jane Grunwald)

Hi Dave,

Can we meet sometime soon to talk about Su Ling? I have some concerns about her. Her progress in English is so slow that I'm beginning to wonder if she has some learning difficulties. I thought it might be useful for you and I to compare notes. We may need to think about a referral to support services. Let me know when it's convenient for you to get together.

Jane

File 19

Mike

After working as a teacher on call for one year with the Lower Valley School District, Diane Thibeault had finally been offered a permanent position at the high school. Her training was in Socials and English, but she also had a music background, which meant that she had worked full-time. Now she'd have her own classes, and would be able to tailor the curriculum to suit her teaching style rather than trying to fit into someone else's mould. She'd be teaching three Grade 9 Socials classes, one Grade 11 English class, and one Grade 12 English class. The only difficulty was that this position had opened up when the original teacher had decided to leave teaching due to illness. Since it was November much of the year's planning had already taken place, including the school-based team meetings.

Diane had substituted for this teacher several times this year already, so she knew quite a few of the students fairly well. The only student who caused some concern was Mike, in Grade 12 English. Mike had cerebral palsy; he used a computer to write and was confined to a wheelchair. When Diane had been the substitute Ms. Hanson, the part-time teacher aide, had pretty much taken care of Mike's work in the class. But now Diane was the teacher responsible for planning and directing all activities in the class. And since Mike would be graduating this year it was important to understand enough about him to know where he was headed in the future.

Ms. Hanson had told Diane that Mike's dream was to become a lawyer like his father. Since Mike apparently had the intellectual capability, she took on the challenge of helping him try to achieve his goal. If she was going to incorporate strategies for Mike so that he'd become an active member of the class she'd first need to know more about his strengths and weaknesses in order to make appropriate decisions. Before she began her unit plan she had to read the entire file.

Mount Lions Secondary School
School-Based Student Support Services

COMPREHENSIVE INDIVIDUAL EDUCATION PLAN

FOR MICHAEL KHATASHAN

Review Date:	May, 1999
Student Name:	Michael Robert Khatashan
DOB:	April 21, 1983
SSS File #:	0-965-2
Case Manager:	Frank LaFontaine

MEMBERS OF THE IEP TEAM

School Principal:	Marilyn Todd
Learning Assistance Teacher:	John Farmer
Occupational Therapist:	Marianne Veloci
Parents:	Andrew and Nancy Khatashan
Student:	Michael Khatashan
Teachers:	Harold Simms, Technical Studies
	Mary Harold, Mathematics
	Francis Moore, Social Studies
	John Monroe, English

Strengths and Interests:

- good listener
- usually happy
- eager to try things
- lets his needs be known
- friendly with other students
- good sense of humour
- cooperative
- knows when something isn't working

Needs:

- increase verbal skills
- increase socialization
- increase self-confidence
- curriculum adapted and modified
- increase work on fine motor skills
- decrease tendency to short-cut work

Learns Best When:

- material is predictable
- material is visually presented
- material is structured from whole to part
- material is presented in a non-stimulating environment
- given extra time to write using computer
- given regular interaction and encouragement from the teacher

Goals:

1. To further develop communication skills

    A. To increase written language

       Suggested Strategies:

- utilize laptop computer more
- encourage spell check regularly
- encourage correct English and spelling
- require complete sentences and paragraphs

    B. To increase visual perception

       Suggested Strategies:

- use stimulation-free materials
- adapt curriculum materials to larger fonts

    C. To increase reading

       Suggested Strategies:

- have Mike outline reading assignments
- develop a base vocabulary journal
- use computer software

    D. To increase verbal ability

       Suggested Strategies:

- allow use of audiotape for reports
- provide opportunity for group work (without aide)
- provide opportunity to initiate conversation

2. To maintain and increase socialization

       Suggested Strategies:

- integrate into regular classes
- TA to use discretion in leaving Mike's side for freer classmate contact
- encourage active participation in classroom activities

Vocational Goals:

    1. To enter the local community college next year

    2. To eventually work his way into law school

McGill Action Plan Results

Grade 8 Participants: Michael, Andrew and Nancy Khatashan—parents, Fr. George Friends—family priest, Noel Zacharey—aunt, Frank Khatashan—older brother

From Michael:

PRESENT GOALS

1. To be more independent with the wheelchair
2. To make friends and to socialize more
3. To gain better control of my hands
4. To work in my father's law office part-time

LONG-TERM GOALS

1. To go to the mall and video store just with my friends
2. To have a job
3. To have my own apartment
4. To have a girlfriend
5. To be independent

DREAMS

1 To drive a car
2. To get married and have a family
3. To travel
4. To become a lawyer like my father

From the Adults:

PRESENT GOALS

1. To have greater access to social activities
2. To increase language and math skills, which would allow him to make career choices
3. To increase his computer skills
4. To allow him to make his own decisions
5. To continue to be happy
6. To continue to have high self-esteem

LONG-TERM GOALS

1. To have as much independence as possible
2. To communicate effectively
3. To develop lasting friendships
4. To find a career that gives him personal satisfaction

DREAMS

1. To be happy
2. To live as normal or regular a life as possible
3. To attain his one goal of becoming a lawyer in his father's office

File 20

Justin

Carla Lupini's Grade 4 classroom was colourful, with learning centres organized around a central area containing small groups of desks. There was a carpeted library corner with a couple of armchairs for children to curl up in, and materials and books were well organized and easily accessible. A strong feeling of cooperation and respect prevailed in the class.

Carla had several students with learning and behavioural challenges. One of them was Justin, who'd been diagnosed as having attention deficit/hyperactivity disorder when he was six. Justin was on Ritalin. His dosage seemed to be appropriate, and Carla knew that his parents were careful to monitor side effects. They were also great about keeping Justin's routine at home predictable, consistent, and organized. Carla's classroom routine was also organized and consistent, but Justin still experienced some challenges at school.

This morning had been tough. Written work usually required extra time for Justin to complete, but today he'd accomplished almost nothing. Spelling and a creative writing assignment were on his homework list for completion. Even Math, on which Justin managed to focus most days and do really well, had been a disaster today. After twenty minutes of searching for his Math book, and another ten for a ruler in his extremely disorganized desk, he'd just lost it. His crying and yelling had upset the other children in his group, and he needed about half an hour to calm down. He'd retreated to his favourite spot, the blue armchair, and curled up with a book. Eventually his sobs subsided and he read the book, a Haida legend, quietly. Then he sat with Carla and told her the story expressively, adding details from his own knowledge of totem poles. He told her enthusiastically about his visit to the anthropology museum. The afternoon was much calmer, as each child designed a mask based on Haida mythology. Justin loved art and was doing an exceptional job on his mask. He worked intently all afternoon and was helpful to others in his group. He left school that afternoon in high spirits.

Carla thought she should review her file on Justin. Maybe it was time to have another chat with Mike, the learning assistance teacher, and see if something needed to be changed in the plan they had worked out to support Justin's spelling and writing development. She also needed to think about how to help keep him organized. There was a psychoeducational report in the file; maybe it would help to have a closer look at it. Justin's parents had had him assessed by a local psychologist in the summer and they'd given her a copy of the report. Because of Justin's variable academic progress through the primary grades they wanted more information on his strengths and weaknesses so that they could be more informed in their approach to helping him at home. Carla put Justin's file in her bag to take home. She'd be able to think more clearly about it after some dinner.

Later Carla made herself comfortable and started to read Justin's file. His intelligence and achievement test scores in the psychoeducational report caught her eye—and she concentrated on those before going over the intervention plan she and Mike had developed last month.

Stanford-Binet Test of Intelligence—Fourth Edition (SB-4)

	SCORE	*PERCENTILE	CLASSIFICATION
Verbal Reasoning	120	89	High Average
Abstract/Visual Reasoning	137	99	Very Superior
Quantitative Reasoning	134	98	Very Superior
Short-Term Memory	127	95	Superior
Total Test Composite	134	98	Very Superior

Woodcock-Johnson Psycho-Educational Battery—Revised (WJ-R): Tests of Achievement—Standard Battery

ACHIEVEMENT CLUSTER	SCORE	PERCENTILE
Broad Reading	134	99
Letter-Word Identification	139	99.5
Passage Comprehension	129	97
Broad Mathematics	147	99.9
Calculation	146	99.9
Applied Problems	141	99.7
Broad Written Language	112	80
Dictation	101	53
Writing Samples	129	97
Broad Knowledge	122	93
Science	129	98
Social Studies	110	74
Humanities	125	95
Skills	129	97

CLASSROOM INTERVENTION PLAN FOR JUSTIN

Date: October 2, 1998

Teacher: <u>Carla Lupini</u>   LAT: <u>Mike Roberts</u>

Strategy	Length of Time Tried	Outcome	Comments
Oral tests	1 month	Great!	Demonstrates his knowledge so much better this way.
Write one sentence at a time in creative writing. Check in with me after each one.	2 weeks	Good. Content isn't as rich as when he dictates a story, but managed four sentences in the museum story today.	Checking in gives him a break and he seems to enjoy talking about story direction. Ready to start two sentences at a time?
Add 2 words of personal interest to class spelling list.	3 weeks	Good for words of interest. Class list still a problem.	Analyze mistakes. Interest an issue or lack of knowledge of some rules??
Checklist of things to do to get ready for work taped to desk.	2 weeks	No change. List is doodled on and barely legible.	
Peer clarifies instructions.	3 weeks	Works some days and not others.	

Justin

I Am good at math And drawing.

Sept. 6/98

The "About Me" activity.
This took 30 minutes to
complete.
            CL

File 21

Dave

John was thrilled to get the teaching job at Franklin Secondary School. It was close to the town where his fiancée worked, and it meant they wouldn't have to move away from their friends once they got married. They were planning a Christmas wedding, and his fiancée's parents were going overboard with the celebration, in his opinion. Anyway, no one really asked him his opinion of the wedding plans so he just went along with whatever Wendy and her mother said.

What concerned him now was a student he knew would be in his Grade 10 Woodworking class. The principal had made sure that John got some information about Dave so that he could plan for September.

Dave Farmer had entered Grade 9 after the family moved down to the city from a northerly First Nations community. Dave suffered from a Traumatic Brain Injury that he'd received after a very bad dirt bike accident in Grade 7. The family had found it difficult to get the medical support Dave required in their town, so it had meant lengthy and costly trips to hospitals. Their Band had paid for a lot of the extras, but the loss of wages when Dave's Dad brought him down had been hard for the family to make up. Finally they'd decided to move closer to the medical support that they knew Dave needed. Since Mr. Farmer was a truck driver he'd had little trouble finding work. According to the counsellor, what was adding stress on the family was the emotional support they missed when they left their community. This had been causing extra problems for Dave, since he was aware that the family problems were the result of the move for him. Now Dave was dealing with bouts of depression on top of the limits set by his injury.

John knew he'd need to understand more about the specifics of Dave's TBI, as well as how to handle his depression. The counsellor had spent some time going over the IEP verbally. Since it was so complex the school had used a shorter form for the teachers, which made the whole thing much more manageable. He'd given John a copy of the form used by the Social Studies teacher last year as an example. The counsellor had also advised John to prepare some questions or issues that he needed help with, since the home–school support worker for the First Nations students would be meeting with them during the first week in September.

IEP SUMMARY FOR THE CLASSROOM TEACHER

Student: _Dave Farmer_

Teacher: _Bob Thornton_

Class: _SS9_ Block: _B_

Date: _Sept. 1997_

OBJECTIVES:

1. Dave will increase his language comprehension.
2. Dave will reduce his impulsiveness.
3. Dave will increase monitoring his own activities.

SUGGESTED STRATEGIES:

1. Use simple language and avoid complex directions.
2. Have Dave repeat directions before he begins a task.
3. Use handouts and notes, as well as audio aids, whenever possible.
4. Try to provide immediate and frequent feedback on tasks.

* Any signs of headaches must be reported to the office immediately.

File 22

Jay

It's interesting how some names become known to teachers even before the students show up in their classes. Jay was one of those students whom everyone on staff knew about. Truancy, mouthing off to teachers, breaking into someone's locker on a dare, leaving tests just as they got started, and leaving the school grounds after getting off the bus to spend the day at the mall were just some of the items on the list. Jay was also suspected of putting the dead snake in the girls' change room after lunch on Monday. Jay was always in some kind of trouble, but the most frustrating thing was that he could be so charming as well. Vicky had been one of those teachers who, despite Jay's' reputation, just couldn't believe he was the same person everyone talked about.

As a Grade 9 English teacher Vicky figured she could handle Jay's behaviour problems. He'd always been polite, and with his good looks and charming smile he seemed to be willing to turn his energy to more productive activities. All that ended abruptly when Vicky learned that it was Jay who'd put oil all over her car windows. He hadn't even tried to do it secretively, but rather showed all the kids how much of a mess you could make with olive oil. When she spoke to Jay about it he apologized and seemed genuinely sorry. However, the next day it happened again.

That day after school the counsellor had a meeting with all of Jay's teachers. Apparently Jay had been in a lot more trouble at home. He'd broken into the neighbour's house while they were away and essentially trashed the kitchen (that's where the olive oil had come from). He was well known to the local police and social services, so this wasn't a surprise to them. There had been considerable effort by the school and social workers to have some testing done to determine the exact nature of Jay's problem, but the testing had always been blocked by Jay's father.

The counsellor had known the family for many years and pretty much understood what was wrong. He shared some very confidential information with them, and requested that the teachers maintain that confidentiality as a personal favour. Jay's mother had been an alcoholic and had gone to a clinic when Jay was two years old. Since then she'd always been supportive of her family, as a loving wife and mother and an avid community volunteer. The father felt there was too much "family baggage" to allow testing or an IEP to be written on Jay. Instead the father had asked the counsellor to see if there was some other way to control Jay in school. The idea was that if he could be controlled in school the same technique might work at home too. That was the reason for the meeting.

The counsellor suggested that a contract be drawn up between the teachers and Jay. His teachers were to write up what they wanted from Jay in their classes, and the counsellor would organize the contract and conditions. The alternative was suspension from school and further involvement with the police and social services.

Vicky now had to figure out what she wanted from Jay and how she was going to deal with him in her classroom. She knew that the last thing she needed was to make an enemy of him, so even with the contract it would be very important to have some ideas and techniques ready to use in class.

To: Ralph Tsortis, Counsellor
From: Vicky McElvy
Re: Jay Thomas
Date: Oct. 14, 1998

Enclosed is the list of behaviours I expect from Jay in English 9.

1. *Must be on time to class.*
2. *Must have books and materials.*
3. *Must complete all in-class and homework assignments.*
4. *Must not interfere or interrupt other students working.*
5. *Must work cooperatively with others during group work.*
6. *Must not leave the room without permission and must come back in a specified time.*

In the past I've found that Jay responds well to the following "rewards" for appropriate behaviour. But these rewards lose their appeal quickly.

1. *Getting to do his work differently from other students, e.g., using coloured paper or writing in point form.*
2. *Getting to go to the library or delivering a message for me.*
3. *Being allowed to give or to read a report first.*

Jay doesn't seem to respond to praise or to appeals for personal satisfaction. While he can be very charming, he doesn't appear to have a desire to please anyone unless it seems to serve his own needs.

P.S. Despite all that's happened I still like Jay. Please let me know how I can help. He's an intelligent young man with a lot of potential, which makes it hard to see him headed in such a self-destructive direction.

File 23

Ryan

It was only the third week of September, but from the beginning Ryan had stood out as one of the leaders in Jeff Kurtz's Grade 4/5 class. Ryan was new to the school and was one of the youngest kids in the class, but he was socially mature. The other children sought his opinion and he seemed to have a remarkable ability to "read" other people and know just how to act in response. Ryan also stood out for his insightful comments in Science, Social Studies, and Language Arts discussions. He had a wonderful ability to make connections and extend his thinking.

Jeff was worried, though. Ryan's stress level during reading and writing activities signalled a problem. Ryan tried valiantly and didn't act out his frustrations the way some children did. He showed remarkable persistence, but whenever reading and writing were required he was clearly not his usual happy, involved self. Jeff didn't have much to go on yet, but what he did have concerned him. He examined his informal assessment of Ryan's oral reading as well as Ryan's "Getting to Know You" writing activity, and pondered the big question of what to try next.

Oral Reading Assessment

Blue Valley Elementary

Name: _Ryan_   Grade _4_

Date: _Sept. 11/98_

Reading selection: _Library book (Gr. 2 level)_

Fluency	Hesitent. Doesn't recognize sentences Stops @ end of each line.
Inflection	OK for sections that were easy for him. Poor when struggling w. decoding
Use of context	Visual: Pictures used for clues. Linguistic: No.
Comprehension[1]	Poor 4/5 literal questions wrong.

HI I AM RYAN.
i LiK pLAib videO Gams
It iS intReSten
i Lik DRAWinG

File 24

Neil

Joanna Franklin sat down at her computer to do some planning for the spring term. Her energy was low after the last few days, but she felt determined to get her planning done. Maybe it would take her mind off today's crisis. Besides, she really needed to enjoy the upcoming spring break without worrying about work. This had been a tough year. There were several children in her Grade 3 class who needed lots of support, but she was most worried about Neil.

Neil was really struggling academically and his behaviour was a constant concern. Problems tended to be cyclical, with periods of relative calm followed by weeks of turmoil. The last few days had been some of the worst for Neil. He looked very tired and distracted and had gotten into several fights a day. After each fight he collapsed in tears, and was slow to recover.

That morning Joanna had begun to understand Neil's difficulties. The school secretary had delivered a message from Neil's neighbour, saying that he'd be late for school and not to ask him why. He arrived just before recess, very quiet and pale, and stayed behind after his classmates ran to the playground. Uncharacteristically, he approached Joanna. Choking back tears, he told her that his mom was in the hospital because his dad had hit her. Joanna could barely control her own tears. She took Neil to the nurse's room and got him settled on the couch while she called the school's childcare worker. Then she asked the principal to take her class for a while after recess.

Bob had arrived shortly and talked quietly to Neil. Joanna was impressed with Bob's sensitive manner with children, and felt glad that the school had such good support. Neil insisted on staying at school, and a neighbour picked him up at 3:00.

As Joanna ran all of this through her head yet again, her resolve to finish her planning evaporated and she gave in to her exhaustion. What could she do to help this little boy? Tomorrow she'd review his file. . . .

Forest Grove Elementary

Report on Progress

Student: Neil Benson

Grade: 3   **Term:** 1

November, 1998

Language Arts

	Exceeds expectations for Grade 3	Meets expectations for Grade 3	Needs development
Expressive Language:			
Expresses him/herself clearly		X	
Participates in oral discussions			X
Listening Skills:			
Listens to others			X
Comprehends and follows instructions			X
Written Language:			
Expresses him/herself clearly in writing		X	
Uses appropriate vocabulary		X	
Writes in sentences		X	
Understands and uses appropriate spelling rules			X
Writes a paragraph using guidelines			X
Edits own work independently			X
Reading:			
Uses phonetic rules appropriately			X
Recognizes sight words		X	
Comprehends what is read			X
Uses context clues in decoding words		X	
Reads for pleasure			X
Reads with purpose			X

Comments:

Neil's written and oral expression are at grade level, and he has some average abilities in reading. Overall, though, Neil needs considerable support in a number of areas of the language arts. He is working on acquiring fundamental spelling and phonetic skills. His comprehension of both oral language and text is weak. We are working on building listening skills. Neil appears to have good reading skills and comprehension. In the classroom, we are working together on building interest in reading.

Social-Emotional Development

G = Good,   **S** = Satisfactory,   **N** = Needs development

Works well with others	N
Plays cooperatively	N
Takes responsibility for own behaviour	N
Manages conflict well	N
Is self-confident	N
Persists with school tasks	N
Is considerate of others	N

Comments:

Neil needs considerable help in getting along with others and with taking responsibility for his work and his behaviour. We are working to support Neil to build positive relationships and self-esteem. Neil has shown periodic improvement in social-emotional development but his growth is inconsistent. He still faces a number of social-emotional challenges.

FOREST GROVE ELEMENTARY

MS. FRANKLIN'S CLASS

November 7, 1998

Dear Mrs. Benson,

We are holding parent meetings during the week of November 21. I will be available before and after school and on Wednesday afternoon. You can schedule an appointment by calling the office at 555-1741. I would be pleased to discuss Neil's progress report and ways in which we can work together to support his development. I look forward to meeting with you.

Sincerely,

Joanna Franklin

☎ TELEPHONE MESSAGE

For: Joanna

From: Marlene Benson 555-6552

Date: November 8   **Time:** 9:15 AM

Please call ___X___   **Will call back** _____

Message

Why do you want to see her? There's nothing wrong with Neil.

(Joanna, she sounds very angry!)

File 25

Carlos

Ken Rossi walked slowly around the periphery of the school playground as he took his turn at recess supervision. The snow glistened on this bright, very cold mid-winter day. Ken noticed Carlos huddled by the door, alone and shivering. He wore a hooded parka, thin cotton pants, and ragged runners. Ken took him inside on the pretext of asking him to help return a stack of books to the library.

Outside again, Ken pondered what to do for Carlos. Carlos and his family had arrived in Canada at the beginning of December, as refugees from Central America. Because Carlos was ten years old he'd been placed in Ken's Grade 5 class, but from what Ken could ascertain this was Carlos's first formal schooling.

Carlos had experienced considerable trauma in his short life. Ken thought that culture shock only added to Carlos's stress—the climate, customs, language, and setting were so vastly different from his experience. From a small village to a metropolis covered in snow—Ken could barely imagine how a young child coped with such massive change. The family's social worker spoke of "cultural fatigue." This term seemed a very appropriate one to describe the impact of circumstances on Carlos.

Ken had taught children with no English before. He was very familiar with periods of withdrawal, acting out of frustration, and the acquisition of a very "colourful" vocabulary at first. With the help of the ESL teacher Carlos was acquiring a functional English vocabulary. The other students were supportive and tried hard to understand and tolerate Carlos's frustration. Ken was pretty proud of how helpful they were in assisting Carlos with oral and written English.

Carlos loved art and music. It was obvious that he hadn't seen crayons, pastels, or paints before, but once he'd discovered their potential he created beautiful work. This won him admiration from the other kids. He also responded sensitively to music. He learned the recorder quickly and participated eagerly in percussion activities.

Carlos's Math skills really puzzled Ken. Carlos had no knowledge of notation, so Ken had rounded up some materials to teach him basic numeracy. But Ken had observed him making change readily in the Math centre on place value, so he'd given him the responsibility of collecting hot dog money from the class. Ken had always seemed to be out a dollar or two, but Carlos excelled at giving the correct change and balancing the account. Ken felt he really needed some guidance in putting all the pieces together to help Carlos develop.

Problem-Based Learning in Inclusive Education

Date: Mon, 18 Jan 1999 16:30:15 (CST)
From: Maria Hernandez <mhernandez@socialservices.on.ca>
To: Ken Rossi <ken.rossi@grovejunior.on.ca>
Subject: Carlos

Hello, Ken.

Things are moving slowly in getting support in place for Carlos's family. The local church has been very helpful in donating bedding, clothes, and some furniture. The family is really struggling. Their preschooler is sick, money is scarce, and the cultural fatigue I mentioned to you is overwhelming. The big challenge is that the family speaks limited Spanish. The language in the home is an Indian dialect. Things move very slowly as I try different ways of conveying meaning in simple Spanish. You might ask your board if they have a support person who has experience with this language issue.

I can help set up a visit with Carlos's parents, but I think we should chat first. They're going to need lots of context to understand the purpose of the meeting. Also, you should probably know more about their background first. I have some good articles that I'll drop off at the school. Thanks so much for your interest and support.

Maria

On Fri, 15 Jan 1999, Ken Rossi wrote:

Maria, thank you very much for dropping by the school before Christmas. Now that Carlos has been at school for a while, I have some more questions. Can you tell me what sort of support the family has? Maybe there's something the school can do to help. Also, I'd really like to meet Carlos's family and tell them how Carlos is progressing (he's got some major talent!). Can you advise me on how to set that up? Thanks for any help you can give.

Ken

Name: carlos

Writing

February 1, 1999

The Class Party

Write about what you would like to do at our class Valentine's party. Think about activities, food, and decorations.

PlY and et
lise musik
colR red

File 26

Hannah and Holly

During the first half-hour of the day in the Grade 2 class children planned their day, then chose an activity for the remaining time. It was a favourite time of day for children and teachers alike—a chance to settle in, get organized for the day, and exercise some personal choice. Team teachers Patty Inglis and Lisa Yamoto valued it because it gave them time to observe the children and to interact informally with them.

Today Lisa observed Hannah and Holly playing with puppets. The twins' identical red ponytails bobbed as they worked their hand puppets in an animated way in the class drama centre. They appeared to have a shared understanding of their dramatic play. To Lisa, though, observing this activity added to her concern about the twins' development. Hannah and Holly's language was immature. They had difficulty understanding prepositional phrases like "behind the door" and "on top of the shelf." They used "on" for "in" and "over" for "in front of." Their vocabulary was limited. Patty was first alerted to just how limited the day Holly asked her if she could borrow "a write with." Vocabulary limitations affected their day-to-day comprehension of class discussions, teacher directions, conversations with peers, and stories. They often interrupted stories to ask, "What's that mean?" The puppet play indicated, once again, that something needed to be done to help with the twins' language development. While Holly and Hannah communicated with each other easily, their ability to communicate with others needed a lot of support.

Patty and Lisa also talked regularly about Hannah and Holly's reading and written language development. In the spring of Grade 2 both girls were struggling with reading material geared for beginning Grade 1 students, and finding written language very difficult. Patty and Lisa wondered how to approach the upcoming parent conference. They wanted to offer some support to Sheila, Hannah and Holly's mother, who tried hard to help out but really had her hands full as a single parent with a toddler at home. But Patty and Lisa worried about how to reinforce the fact that the girls needed more exposure to language. When they had met with Sheila in the fall she'd been so proud of the fact that the girls had each other to talk to, and appeared to dismiss their concerns about language development.

In addition to offering the right kind of support to Sheila, Patty and Lisa were wondering where to turn next themselves. Hannah and Holly had learning assistance support, but what more could be done?

Student Background

Name: Hannah Page

Age: 7

Address: 62 Ryder Lane #201

Phone: 555-0011

Mother's Name Sheila Lundquist

Address
(if different from above)

Work: _____ **Home:** 555-0011

Father's Name Ted Page

Address Unknown
(if different from above)

Work: _____ **Home:** _____

Legal Guardian _____

Work: _____ **Home:** _____

Family Information: Younger brother, age 2

School	Year	Grade	Placement
Rivercrest Elementary	1996-97	K	Full day
Rivercrest Elementary	1997-	1	Multi-age K-2
Pearson Elementary	1998	1	1/LAC 1x/wk.
Pearson Elementary	1998-99	2	2/LAC 3x/wk.

Problem-Based Learning in Inclusive Education

Medical History: _Normal development reported_

by mother.

Healthy

Medications: _None_

Student Background

Name: Holly Page

Age: 7

Address: 62 Ryder Lane #201

Phone: 555-0011

Mother's Name Sheila Lundquist

Address
(if different from above)

Work: _____ **Home:** 555-0011

Father's Name Ted Page

Address Unknown
(if different from above)

Work: _____ **Home:** _____

Legal Guardian _____

Work: _____ **Home:** _____

Family Information: Younger brother, age 2

School	Year	Grade	Placement
Rivercrest Elementary	1996-97	K	Full day
Rivercrest Elementary	1997-	1	Multi-age K-2
Pearson Elementary	1998	1	1/LAC 1x/wk.
Pearson Elementary	1998-99	2	2/LAC 3x/wk.

Medical History: Normal development reported by mother.
Healthy.

Medications: None.

Formal Assessments

Type	Evaluator	Date
PPVT-R	Lana Van Dyck (LAC)	May 12, 1998

Result 79th. percentile

Type	Evaluator	Date
Woodcock-Johnson	Lana Van Dyck (LAC)	May 19, 1998

Result
Letter-word identification 81 (10th percentile)
Word attack 76 (5th percentile)
Passage comprehension 82 (12th percentile)

Type	Evaluator	Date

Result

Type	Evaluator	Date

Result

Holly P.
Div. 16

Formal Assessments

Type	Evaluator	Date
PPVT-R	Lana Van Dyck (LAC)	May 12, 1998

Result		
79th percentile		

Type	Evaluator	Date
Woodcock-Johnson	Lana Van Dyck (LAC)	May 19, 1998

Result		
Letter-word identification	77	(6th percentile)
Word attack	70	(2nd percentile)
Passage comprehension	85	(16th percentile)

Type	Evaluator	Date

Result		

Type	Evaluator	Date

Result		

Portfolio Reflections

Student Name: _Hannah_   Date: _Nov 14/98_

I was pleased that my child

Writes

Draws

Knows numbers

Questions I have about my child's progress:

Parent/Guardian Signature: _Sheila L._

Portfolio Reflections

Student Name: _Holly_   Date: _Nov 14/98_

I was pleased that my child

Writes

Knows numbers

Questions I have about my child's progress:

Where is her drawing?

Parent/Guardian Signature: _Sheila L._

File 27

Rusty

Fran Di Lucca threw her bag of exercise books on the back seat of her car. She settled into the driver's seat, congratulated herself on a relatively smooth day with Rusty, and started for home. She taught and lived in a small suburban community and her drive home took about twenty minutes—just enough time to begin to unwind. Today she reflected on her relationship with Rusty, the oldest but smallest boy in her Grade 5 class. In a nutshell, the year had been like a roller coaster ride.

Rusty had arrived in early October and immediately upset the cohesiveness of her class. He was aggressive and defiant, and intimidated the other children. Fran herself occasionally felt like running and hiding but had stood her ground, even in the face of abusive language. She fielded constant reports of theft from her other students, none of which could be proved. Her principal dealt with complaints about vandalism from neighbouring households, but there was no conclusive evidence that Rusty was to blame. Rusty had acquired a reputation quickly and now, in the spring, that reputation seemed permanent.

On the other hand, Rusty often seemed so desperate to do well in school. He had incredible difficulty with reading and his written work was typical of emergent writing. He went to the LAC for support every day. He worked well there, as he did with a parent volunteer who helped him with reading. Fran modified the amount of reading and writing expected of him, had him tape-record some work, and included a variety of high interest/low vocabulary books in all the learning centres. His mom helped with reading at home when she could, but she had a lot of challenges herself and Fran tried to take that into consideration.

As long as he was focused and well supported, Rusty coped academically. However, school life was a constant challenge for both Rusty and Fran. Rusty reacted swiftly and angrily to academic frustration and perceived threats. Fran had yet to figure out if there was a pattern to the triggers that set him off. When a day passed calmly as it had today, Fran was relieved to have the challenges go away for a while.

About halfway home Fran spotted Rusty riding his bike in the same direction. "What on earth?" she thought as she passed this small boy steering his bike with his left hand and balancing another bike under his right arm.

BETH KLINE
26 Creekside Lane
Centreville, MN

April 7, 1999

Dear Ms. Di Lucca,

Jonathan came home today in tears, yet again. He has such a terrible time coping with Rusty's bullying. I really am at the point where I feel some action needs to be taken. It simply isn't right that one child can influence other children's lives so negatively. School life for Jonathan has gone from enthusiastic to fearful. I know he isn't the only one who's intimidated. I've talked to several of the other parents, and we've agreed to take this to the school board. I understand how difficult this situation is for you as well, but after the number of complaints we've registered with your principal we feel this is the next logical alternative.

Sincerely,

Beth Kline

Fran Di Lucca   4:15 PM   03/31/99   Concern

Date: Wed, 31 Mar 1999   16:15:30
Subject: Concern
To: Fran Di Lucca<fdilucca@centreville.sd17.mn.ca>
From: <ctravis@centreville.sd17.mn.ca > (Cynthia Travis)

Hi Fran,

Sorry to lay this on you at the end of the day. I just had quite the altercation with Rusty. He was throwing rocks at the children waiting for the bus. When I confronted him he told me he wasn't on school property and there was nothing I could do to him! I insisted it was my responsibility because I had to look out for our pupils' safety. This resulted in language I won't repeat, after which he grabbed his bike and rode off. The other kids were pretty shaken up.

I told Frank about this and he's calling Rusty's mom. Thought you should hear from me as well.

Cindy

CONFERENCE NOTES

Student: <u>Rusty Miles</u>   **Parent:** <u>Lynn Miles</u>   **Date:** Nov. 2/98

Pre-report Conference First Term

Expressed concerns about R's academic achievement and behaviour. Talked over strategies to help with both and tried to get mom's perspective on what works at home. Explained our book-lending program; suggested some good choices for R; asked Lynn if she or another family member would be able to read with R at home.

Lynn explained the following circumstances that affect R:

- Dad is in prison.
- She's on parole. R's aunt and grandmother shared childcare responsibilities over the last three years.
- L. is trying hard to put the pieces together.

Asked if she'd like to come to a school-based team meeting with me to talk over support for R. *Very* hesitant (Qs: Who's there? How long? What might happen? What will they ask me?). Tried to reassure, but will have to go slowly on this one.

Plan: Try reading with R once or twice a week. Meet again next month.

*Appointments made for Dec. 2 and Jan. 15 both missed.

File 28

Samantha

Greg Smyth prided himself on his strong record of helping children with special needs. He chaired the school-based team, and was close to finishing a master's degree in Special Education. He'd chosen to work in the primary grades because he felt he could make more of a difference there. In his ten years of teaching he had acquired a good reputation for his knowledge of special education and his innovative, supportive approaches to teaching. Greg felt less than successful with Samantha, though. This little girl in his Grade 2 class was so keen to learn, but her low vision resulted in a number of challenges.

Greg had some general knowledge of the impact of low vision. He worked closely with the district's itinerant teacher, Sharon Grant, to try to balance Samantha's exposure to both print and Braille. Unfortunately, Sharon's responsibilities extended over a large district where travel between schools was extensive. In a good month, Sharon managed two visits. Greg and one of the school's special education assistants tried to follow up on Sharon's suggestions between visits. Neither of them was familiar enough with Braille, though, to really make this work. Greg also knew that he needed to find out a good deal more about the impact of low vision on print literacy.

Greg recognized that much more expertise was necessary to help Samantha develop. His discussion with her parents had centred on their mutual concern about her low academic achievement and the appropriate balance of print and Braille instruction. He'd been glad to hear that they had pursued an independent assessment. He sat down to read the report and plan for the next team meeting. It was time to make some strong recommendations for next year.

Name: Samantha Greene

Birth Date: July 2, 1989

Age: 8 years, 10 months

Parents: Thomas and Philipa Greene

Telephone: 555-1634

Address: 1177 Laurel Avenue

Long Lake, SK

Date of Evaluation: May 27 & 28, 1998

Date of Report: June 26, 1998

Grade: 2

PURPOSE OF ASSESSMENT

The purpose of the assessment was to assess Samantha's learning media needs and to provide recommendations for instructional programming.

BACKGROUND INFORMATION

Samantha Greene is completing Grade 2. She has received instruction in both print and Braille, but her parents are concerned that she's not making appropriate progress in either medium. According to the referral for the current evaluation, the educational team has been struggling over the issue of whether to provide instruction in print, Braille, or both. However, records suggest that a decision has been made on Samantha's reading media. The clinical low vision report dated 4-14-98 stated: "It is expected that Braille will become her primary literacy medium in the near future." Also, a report by the district vision teacher Vivian Levesque stated: "Samantha's educational team determined at the end of her kindergarten year that she should receive instruction to learn Braille."

The parents provided a copy of Samantha's latest achievement scores from the *Canadian Tests of Basic Skills*. The results indicated that Samantha was generally achieving academically in the low range as compared with other children in Grade 2 without visual impairments. There were several areas in which Samantha was performing in the high range, including initial sounds and several areas of listening skills. However, since a live reader apparently read portions of the tests to Samantha, it's uncertain whether these results represent her true level of academic achievement. It's likely that informal measures used by her teacher and others will provide better indicators of achievement.

According to the Low Vision Clinic report by Dr. Cynthia Woreck dated 5-11-98, Samantha has a history of macular hypoplasia, optic nerve pallor, and high myopia. Her distance visual acuity was 20/250 with correction and 20/400 without correction. Her near visual acuity was 1M print at one inch with or without correction. No low vision devices were prescribed. Dr. Woreck concluded, "Samantha's vision is limited, particularly for near point activities."

ASSESSMENT RESULTS

Use of Sensory Channels

General observation of Samantha's use of her sensory channels reveals that she uses vision as a primary sensory channel and touch and hearing as secondary channels. However, when demanding tasks are completed at near point, such as reading, her efficiency in use of vision decreases dramatically. Therefore, it's not possible to link her general level of sensory functioning at distance to any recommendation of literacy media. Such a recommendation must consider efficiency in completing print reading tasks, as indicated in the next section.

Print Reading Skills

Samantha's print reading skills were evaluated by using the *John's Basic Reading Inventory*. This instrument has short passages of increasing difficulty and accompanying comprehension questions. Samantha read passages in large print (18-point type) and with the closed-circuit television (CCTV).

Samantha read the pre-primer passage aloud in large print at a rate of 11 words per minute with 100% comprehension. She used a working distance of about 1 inch from the page. Her reading was slow and laboured and lacked fluency. She spent a great deal of time attempting to sound out words, with little regard for contextual information. Often sounding out the words did not allow her to eventually say the word correctly. When Samantha was asked to reread this same passage with the CCTV, her rate increased to 29 words per minute. While part of this increase in rate must be attributed to familiarity with the passage, it was clear that the CCTV helped Samantha to read print materials more easily. Her posture was normal and relaxed, she tracked materials efficiently, and her working distance was increased.

On the primer passage, Samantha read with the CCTV at a distance of 8 inches from the screen. She read at 14 words per minute and with 90% comprehension. Again, it was noted that the CCTV allowed her to read more comfortably. While her comprehension of this passage was very good, her unassisted word recognition accuracy was below the frustration level. Again, Samantha attempted to sound out many unknown words, often unsuccessfully.

At the beginning of the second day of the assessment, Samantha was asked to read a Grade 1 passage. She sat somewhat closer to the CCTV for this passage and worked at a distance of 4 to 5 inches from the screen. Samantha read this passage at a rate of 20 words per minute and with 80% comprehension. Her word recognition accuracy was at the frustration level.

In addition to passage reading, Samantha was administered the word recognition section of the *John's Basic Reading Inventory*. At the pre-primer level, she recognized 95% of a list of 20 words; this was her independent level. Her accuracy at the primer level was 70% and at the Grade 1 level, 50%; these grades would be considered her frustration level. Throughout this portion of the assessment, as well as the passage reading, it was noted that Samantha attempted to sound out many high-frequency words that she should know instantly.

A technique called Paired Reading was used in a diagnostic teaching session in an effort to encourage Samantha to read more fluently. In this technique, a skilled reader (usually a teacher or parent) first reads a short passage aloud to provide a model for a less skilled reader. Then the student reads the same passage. When Paired Reading was used with a short narrative passage, Samantha's reading fluency increased noticeably and immediately. Given that Samantha's usual pattern is to sound out many words in passage, use of techniques like Paired Reading will allow her to better know what fluent reading should sound like.

Braille Reading and Writing Skills

To assess Samantha's Braille reading and writing skills the examiners used a variety of activities. Samantha was asked to read Braille from a twin-vision book that her parents supplied. She also participated in a cooperative reading activity with the examiner in which Samantha read one page, the examiner read the next, then Samantha, then the examiner, and so forth. When the examiner was reading Samantha was asked to place her fingers on the Braille cells that were being read.

Finally, Samantha was asked to write Braille using a Perkins Braillewriter. During the second day the examiner used a diagnostic teaching approach to determine Samantha's ability to learn new strategies for reading Braille.

Samantha consistently demonstrated scrubbing and backtracking while reading Braille, and she did not exhibit basic hand movement skills, such as efficient use of two hands on a Braille line. She continued to use the same method of "sounding out" words in Braille that she used in print. Samantha knew a few Braille contractions, but could not read continuous text in authentic literature in Braille because she didn't have an adequate knowledge of Braille contractions and couldn't use context cues to determine those symbols that she didn't automatically know. In general, Samantha's existing Braille reading skills do not allow efficient use of the medium, even for a beginning reader. It's clear that Samantha's Braille reading instruction has been woefully inadequate, which has resulted in an overall lack of progress in this area.

When asked to write in Braille, Samantha placed her hands on the Braillewriter in the correct position and was able to produce Braille letters upon demand. Her Braille writing skills were limited by her lack of knowledge of the Braille code.

During the second day of this examination, Samantha participated in activities designed to determine her ability to progress in Braille. First, the examiner presented Samantha with word groups (say, day, pay, may…; cat, hat, mat, pat…). After a very short period of time, Samantha was able to more quickly read through the list of words looking only at the beginning letter and recognizing the word by using the context of the word group and the initial letter cue. Second, Samantha was asked to read a new passage of text. Prior to the beginning of the reading activity, the examiner discussed with Samantha the idea that she should sound out any unfamiliar word in her head and then just say the final version of the word after she had thought about it silently. It was the examiner's opinion that Samantha thought that one of the rules of reading was that the teacher needed to hear her thought process. By explaining to Samantha that the examiner only wanted the final version of the word, she was allowed the freedom to use other methods of getting to the final version without relying only on dissecting the word phonetically.

Samantha's progress during this second session was quite impressive and led the examiners to believe that with intense, daily instruction, Samantha could make remarkable progress and become a good Braille reader. She was highly motivated to perform the tasks that were asked of her, and she was successful in trying to implement the examiner's suggestions. She still had difficulty with reading during the second day because of her limited knowledge of the Braille code, but she demonstrated a keen ability to progress in her use of context clues during this second reading experience.

Handwriting

Samantha completed a variety of handwriting activities, both in formal assessment situations and during informal times. She always used manuscript writing and tried a variety of felt-tip markers of various colours. Samantha's handwriting is very legible and neat and provides an efficient means of communicating with classroom teachers and others. She can also read back her handwriting, although this is a slow and often inefficient process.

Literacy Tools

Samantha has started developing a variety of literacy tools, including use of the CCTV, keyboarding skills, and listening skills. As noted previously, Samantha has good skills in using the CCTV for reading. She can adjust the size of letters and the contrast to best meet her individual needs. Her tracking of materials is good, though she tended to prefer having the X-Y table in a fixed position and "scooting" the materials on top of the table. Samantha's efficiency with the CCTV could be improved by using the X-Y table in a conventional manner. Samantha is also able to use the CCTV for handwriting purposes; however, her handwriting skills in general are quite good without use of the CCTV.

Samantha also demonstrated basic keyboarding skills using a laptop computer with large letters on the screen. She was observed placing her fingers correctly on the home row keys and using proper finger movements in striking keys. She would often attempt to look at the keys when searching for particular letters. Part of this may be due to the fact that she was using a laptop computer that was unfamiliar to her. Also, it's not uncommon to find students searching for keys at the early stages of learning keyboarding skills. We believe that Samantha will continue to develop and improve her keyboarding skills with consistent instruction and practice and that, eventually, word processing skills will offer her a valuable and efficient means of written communication.

In order to assess listening skills Samantha listened to passages that were read aloud from the *Burns and Roe Informal Reading Inventory* and then responded to comprehension questions. Her listening comprehension was 100% for the Grade 1 passage, 50% for the Grade 2 passage, and 75% for the Grade 3 passage. The examiners felt that these findings did not represent Samantha's true level of listening skills, since the passages that were read and the questions that were asked were not altogether typical of literature at the early grade levels. The listening subtest of the *Canadian Tests of Basic Skills* is probably a better indicator of Samantha's listening skills. These results indicate that she performed in the high range compared with her Grade 2 classmates in predicting outcomes, following directions, and spatial relationships. She was average in the areas of inferential meaning and visual relationships. Overall, the results of the CTBS suggest that listening skills are a relative strength for Samantha, which supports the examiners' informal observations.

DISCUSSION

Samantha is an energetic and conscientious student who is eager to learn and to try new tasks. Her sensory profile is somewhat complex in that she appears to be a strong visual learner, but her visual skills do not allow an efficient way for her to complete the demanding task of print reading. The lack of print reading efficiency is clearly supported by the low reading rates that were found in this assessment. She read new passages at a rate between 14 and 20 words per minute with the CCTV; her rate with large print materials was even lower at 11 words per minute. Her classmates without visual impairments typically read at a minimum oral reading rate of about 70 words per minute, which places Samantha at a significant disadvantage in keeping up with her classmates in schoolwork related to reading. While it's possible and likely that some of this discrepancy is related to inconsistent reading instruction, it's clear to the examiners that even with the best instruction, her visual condition will negatively influence adequate progress in an *exclusive* print reading program. However, print reading and writing will be valuable tools for Samantha, and she should continue to receive instruction in print literacy skills.

We were pleased to see Samantha's response to the Braille literacy activities that were presented in diagnostic teaching sessions during the assessment. She was eager and excited to read stories in Braille when given instruction, support, and encouragement from a qualified and experienced educator. She possesses rudimentary hand movement skills, discrimination skills, and letter/word recognition skills, but is performing these skills at a level that is lower than would be expected given her abilities and interests. We believe that this lack of progress can be attributed largely to the inconsistent and infrequent Braille literacy instruction that has been provided.

From Samantha's standpoint, she's made good progress given the amount of instruction that has been offered to her. What is clear to us, though, is that she can make much better progress with daily, intense, and quality Braille literacy instruction from a qualified teacher of students with visual impairments.

Samantha's overall approach to reading at this point seems to be one of sounding out words in an attempt to read words and sentences. She has some basic phonics skills, but they're insufficiently integrated into her general strategies for reading. That is, she provides the sounds to letters, but does not integrate the individual sounds into a whole that makes a meaningful word. It appears that the instruction provided only one part of the strategy for using phonetic cues. One key focus of instruction should be to encourage Samantha to use more contextual information to attack unknown words rather than relying on use of phonetic cues. Another focus should be to teach high frequency words to the automatic recognition level. However, these two subskills represent only a small portion of a comprehensive literacy program that must balance and incorporate mechanical skills (hand movements, line change skills, page turning skills), tactual perception skills, vocabulary skills, word recognition skills, comprehension skills, and so forth. These Braille reading skills will need to be integrated seamlessly with a quality and sequential program in print literacy skills. The careful balancing and integration of print and Braille media that will be required to maximize Samantha's progress in literacy development will require the expertise and creativity of a skilled, qualified teacher of students with visual impairments. Alternative patterns to address Samantha's needs, such as the use of a paraprofessional or an educator who's not experienced and qualified to teach students with visual impairments, will fail to adequately address Samantha's identified needs.

The approach that the educational team uses to teach reading and writing skills to Samantha in both print and Braille must be holistically and thoughtfully developed, and professionally and systematically implemented. We're not convinced that the use of *Patterns* is the best approach to use for teaching Braille literacy skills, since it precludes seamless integration with a print literacy program. That is, *Patterns* was designed exclusively for use by beginning Braille readers and can't be used (or shouldn't be used) as an approach to teach print literacy skills. Therefore, whole language methods—as currently used in Samantha's general classroom—would provide the teacher with an approach designed for print readers that could readily be adapted for use by Braille readers. Samantha would have the motivational aspects of using pictures to supplement and reinforce the reading process, as well as authentic literature to practise both print and Braille literacy skills. The report by Catherine Wong, a vision consultant for the province dated 3-1-97, provides an excellent and well-thought-out discussion of the issues surrounding literacy programming for Samantha. We encourage the education team to use this report as the basis for developing and implementing a literacy program for Samantha; we will not repeat the information here.

A decision to teach Samantha both print and Braille must be made definitely and immediately. The delay in making this decision has already resulted in fragmentation of her current literacy program, which we believe has significantly interfered with her rate of achievement. Also, any further delay may cause Samantha to begin to question the value of Braille. That is, she may feel that Braille merits less status or value when compared to print, because the adults in her life can't decide whether it's a good or bad thing to teach her. We're very pleased to see that Samantha's attitude toward Braille is still positive, but we're concerned about any continued indecision on the part of the educational team.

We wish to conclude this discussion with one final thought. There is no hesitation or reservation whatsoever on our part as to the need for Samantha to learn lit-

Problem-Based Learning in Inclusive Education

eracy in both print and Braille. We feel that the only point of discussion is how best to implement a cohesive, holistic, and quality literacy program to adequately address Samantha's unique and individual needs.

RECOMMENDATIONS

1. **Implement literacy instruction for Samantha in both print and Braille.** We recommend that the educational team make a firm decision and commitment to teaching Samantha both print (with the CCTV) and Braille literacy skills. Given that Samantha's reading achievement is lagging behind that of her classmates, we recommend that a qualified teacher of students with visual impairments take primary responsibility for implementing the total literacy program. This will allow one teacher to have the responsibility for assuring that all aspects of Samantha's literacy program are appropriately balanced and integrated between the two media. It will also provide an opportunity for one teacher to maximize the instructional time. For example, in teaching new vocabulary words the teacher can reinforce recognition of the words alternating in print and Braille or Braille and print. The actual teaching of vocabulary (word meanings) per se need not be repeated, as this is a psychological and conceptual process that's largely independent of the medium by which words are conveyed. Also, when the teacher is providing guided reading throughout the story, a portion of the story can be read in Braille and another portion can be read in print (or vice versa). If two reading strategy lessons are provided in direct instruction in a given day, one can be presented in print and the other in Braille. There is no need to repeat each activity in each medium. Throughout the day the classroom teacher should provide a balance of activities in Braille and print in collaboration with a qualified teacher of students with visual impairments.

2. **Provide at least two hours each day of integrated and coordinated instruction in print and Braille literacy instruction by a qualified teacher of students with visual impairments.** Samantha needs at least as much, if not more, instructional time in developing literacy skills as her classmates without visual impairments. We believe that two hours daily is an appropriate amount of specialized instructional time to be provided by a qualified teacher of students with visual impairments. This block of daily time, at a minimum, will allow the teacher to address Samantha's needs in both print and Braille and to coordinate and integrate the instruction between the two media.

3. **Use the CCTV as the primary mode of print reading.** Based on our observations and assessment results, reading print with the CCTV is the most comfortable and efficient means of reading print for Samantha. Reading large print alone appears to be quite limiting for her. Therefore, we recommend that a CCTV be placed in the classroom and that a qualified teacher of students with visual impairments integrate efficient use of the device with the teaching of print reading and, as appropriate, print writing. While we recommend that a CCTV be used as a primary mode of print reading, this does not or should not preclude the use of unaided reading when that is deemed most appropriate or when chosen by Samantha.

4. **Place primary emphasis on literary Braille at this point; continue to use print as the primary medium for mathematics.** Implementing a literacy program in both print and Braille will require a balance of emphasis between the two media. We feel that it's reasonable and appropriate to continue with print in her math class and delay the introduction of the Nemeth Code until Samantha's literary Braille skills are better established. It would be appropriate and helpful to provide some early *exposure* to the Nemeth code—such as writing, numerals, and possibly simple equations—to let Samantha know that there are differences between the codes used for conventional literature and mathematics.

5. **Do not overcorrect miscues in Samantha's oral reading.** We recommend that teachers avoid overcorrecting Samantha's miscues when they don't interfere with the meaning. This approach will allow Samantha to focus more on the meaning of the story rather than on the sounds of the letters in the words.

6. **Increase Samantha's use of contextual cues to attack unknown words.** There's a wide variety of teaching strategies, such as the many variations of the cloze procedure, that can be used to increase Samantha's use of contextual cues in reading print and Braille. We recommend that such strategies be used to help Samantha focus more on using the meaning generated from the sentences to help her recognize unknown words.

7. **Use targeted strategies for increasing Samantha's reading fluency.** During the assessment the examiners used a technique called Paired Reading to assess its impact on Samantha's reading efficiency; it provided immediate results. There is a variety of similar techniques, some of which are described in the appendix of *Learning Media Assessment of Students with Visual Impairment: A Resource Guide for Teachers* (published by the Texas School for the Blind and Visually Impaired). We recommend that one technique be selected and used consistently with Samantha over an extended period of time (e.g., at least one school year). Reading rates should be plotted on a line chart to ensure that there are direct effects from using the technique. Techniques to increase fluency can be used with equal success in print and Braille.

8. **Teach high-frequency words to the automatic level.** We recommend that Samantha receive drill and practice instruction in the instant recognition of high-frequency words. The Dolch 200 word list is commonly used for this purpose.

9. **Continue to teach keyboarding skills to Samantha.** Samantha should continue to receive keyboarding instruction on a consistent basis. As soon as possible, she needs to begin using a simple word processing program to allow her another option (in addition to handwriting) for completing written communication tasks.

10. **Use paraprofessional assistance judiciously.** A qualified teacher of students with visual impairments must take primary responsibility for direct instruction in literacy skills for Samantha. While strict practice in oral reading may be facilitated by others (parents, classroom volunteers, paraeducators), this should be limited, and all the people who listen to Samantha read should be instructed on the importance of allowing her to use context cues and not encouraging her to "sound out" all the words in a reading passage. Paraeducators could also be used to assist the classroom teacher and teacher of students with visual impairments in preparing classroom materials and recreational reading materials for Samantha. A paraeducator must never be given the responsibility to introduce new literacy skills to Samantha.

It was a pleasure for us to work with Samantha and to talk with her parents during this assessment. If there are any questions concerning this report, please contact Edward Freeman at 555-0078 or Nicola Hastings at 555-2562.

Edward Freeman

Edward Freeman, Ed.D.
Associate Professor
Long Lake College

Nicola Hastings

Nicola Hastings, Ph.D.
Professor
The University of the North

File 29

Kevin

When Sue's husband Ted had brought up the possibility of the mining company he worked for moving them to the Northwest Territories, she had been delighted. Both of them were avid camping, fishing, and general sports nuts so this was a great opportunity. Sue had taught for two years, and had just finished a Diploma in Special Education. The move had gone smoothly and she'd quickly made friends in this small community.

Her Grade 10 English class had been going well during the past two months, but now it was time to really give some thought to Kevin. With his dark hair and complexion and his large eyes she knew he was the topic of most of the girls' conversations in the hall. But Kevin seemed oblivious to all this adoration from the girls. Instead he apparently spent a considerable amount of time figuring out ways to end up in the office or in detention after school. It was a shame that Kevin was seen as a troublemaker, since he had a number of excellent qualities that Sue thought were overlooked because of his behaviour.

Sue had surreptitiously observed him last week when she had lunchtime hallway duty. It was as if he couldn't stand and talk to his friends without his hands finding trouble. She watched him at the other end of the hall talking to two other boys. The janitor had left an old cabinet in the hall that needed repair for a wobbly leg. Kevin started to gently rock the cabinet while continuing to talk to his friends. It was as if he wasn't even aware of what he was doing. Before Sue could make it through the crush of students the leg broke and the entire thing fell over with a deafening crash. The principal was angry, and even more furious when it was obvious that Kevin had been the one to make it go over. It was fortunate that Sue had been watching and saw that it wasn't deliberate, otherwise Kevin would have been in deep trouble—again.

Sue knew that Kevin was a bright young man with a wonderful sense of humour. But on top of his continual presence in the principal's office Kevin was having trouble with most of his classes. He was capable of bringing some insights into their discussions in English class that went far beyond the type of work he handed in for assignments. The essay on *To Kill a Mockingbird* was a good example. In class he'd been able to ask, as well as answer, thoughtful questions regarding plot and character development. He'd been particularly interested in the cultural issues portrayed in the story, as had the whole class. But when it came to writing something up about the novel the results were disappointing.

Since Sue had a special education background she was asked to participate as a member of the school-based team. It seemed that the team worked most afternoons after school to deal with students already identified as needing assistance. This made it even more important to collect as much information as possible on Kevin before she brought up his name to the team. Sue discovered that Kevin had burned a lot of bridges with a number of teachers, which made it difficult for them to get past the behaviour and really look at his work.

Since many of the students, including Kevin, were from the Dogrib Nation, Sue wanted to be sure that she'd be able to communicate with parents and the community. Sue had asked Marie Zoe, the teacher's aide, to help her with some of the Dogrib words. She was reassured when Marie Zoe told her that there were descriptions in Dogrib to coincide with special education terms. During her studies she'd heard many debates about the issue of characteristics being culturally derived rather than innate.

The school counsellor had been helpful too. Since he was in regular contact with Kevin's parents about schoolwork he had some useful knowledge and insights. Because Sue was interested only in Kevin's schoolwork and not the conduct issues her file was very small, but it was a place to start.

To: Sue Thiebeault
From: Ed Todd
Date: Nov. 3, 1998
RE: Kevin Janus

At your request I've contacted Kevin's parents. They're always helpful, but I think they've had it with Kevin. His father had hoped Kevin would go to university, as he did. (Mr. Janus is a civil engineer who's very active in local Band affairs.)

Anyway, Kevin has seen their doctor within the past year and is in good health. (It was hard to explain why we wanted that information, since it didn't have anything to do with his recent behaviour.)

At least two of his teachers feel that his behaviour reflects indifference and that his schoolwork shows a lack of motivation. Regina Clarke was interested in your thoughts and sent along a copy of one of Kevin's Social Studies assignments that was done in class (it's not graded). The assignment was to write a ten-minute speech to convince the people of PEI to join Confederation.

Hope this helps.

P.S. His parents had a hard time last year getting him back to school after his suspension for pulling the fire alarm. It seems to be an uphill battle at home.

Dear Sue,

After our conversation I had to speak to several Elders to make sure I had the right word in Kwakwala and Dogrib. The literal translation may not be exactly like Special Education terminology, but the words are very close and the intent is the same.

<u>*Kwakwala terms:*</u>

English	Kwakwala	Literal translation back to English
gifted	nogad	"smart"
hyperactive	xwilasa	"fidgety"
attention deficit	wokwo` goye`	"bum itchy"
behaviour disorder	hat'alalkw	"disobedient"
intellectually delayed	awinagamala	"slow"
language difficulty	taxwamala k'ayud	"hard time talking"
speech difficulty	k'ak'idzakwala	"doesn't say things right"
deaf	gwalkwam	"deaf"
blind	p'ap'as	"blind"
learning disability	awabala	"slow to learn"
physical disability	ye'gamnukw	"something wrong with you"

<u>*Dogrib terms:*</u>

special needs students	t'asìi t'à gihoeɂaa
gifted	do / chekoa t'asìi t'à n'à ghòò
slow learner, intellectually delayed	įghà t'asìi niedì-le
deaf	t'saìi t'a wedzìi goìlee
behaviour disorder	do ladi xè whedaa k'èezo-le
language delay	įghà yati kèhoezo-le
learning disability	t'asìi wehoe a t'à hoghàweeto ha dìi
physical disability	t'asìi tà wehoeɂaa
achievement	t'saìi k'e hatsįįlàà sìi
blind	nezįį wegha xegaat'į -le
attention deficit/ hyperactivity disorder	ts'èhwhįį t'asìi daà niwo ha dìi / chokoa goye
allergies	t'asìi gogha nezįį-le wet'à eyats'įįlįį

I think this will make it much easier to speak to people in the community. Let me know if there's any other way I can help.

Cheers,

Marie Zoe

To Kill a Mockingbird   Kevin Jarvis
                                         English 10

A story which should be preserved for the future
is To Kill a Mockingbird. I think people of the future
would be fascinated by the characters.

I think that people should know how other people
treat each other. People would be interested in how other
people think back then. It would teach what human
behavior was like back then.

The part I liked best was the Radley House
and Mr. Radley. He sounds like he was a strange. They
didn't go to church. Nobody liked them. Scout thought
they were spookie

Name: Kevin Jarvis

Block: B - SS 10

Write a ten minute speech convincing the people of Prince Edward
Island to join the other colonies and sign the Confederation.

Prince Edward Island should become one of the parts
of Canada. It is important to sign the confederation. It is
good for your future. And your children. With the six colonies
we can have better defense against our enemys. You will feel
th power of a country that is whole. We can stand and be
not pushed by our neighbors. We will be happy. We can help
each other in bad times. It is good for our all people. Please
sign the confederation so we can be happy.

File 30

Anna

Anna was one of those students who come along infrequently, thank goodness. The problem wasn't her schoolwork so much as her difficult personality. Mark Whitman had trouble even talking to her some days. He wanted to help her succeed in English 8, but at times it was a real trial. At this large regional secondary school it was easy for the Grade 8s to become lost in the system, and as a result their teachers were responsible for monitoring their progress more closely than that of the older students. The principal was adamant that any new student with a problem would not be overlooked.

Anna was fitting into the profile of a student with problems. She had a way of flipping her hair and looking at you with a smug expression that relayed an unspoken rudeness. It was as if she knew that her look would infuriate adults, which it did. And since her attitude was conveyed primarily through body language it made it very hard to explain to anyone who hadn't worked with Anna. Often Mark caught himself just as he was ready to tell her to take that look off her face. (He couldn't believe he was using his mother's phrase!) Control was the answer, but his was running out and he knew he'd have to do something soon.

Mark was positive that Anna did it deliberately. When he sat at the table at the back of the room—his "help desk" as he told his class—Anna would wait until she had an audience and then make a show of what she thought about his suggestions. The bothersome thing was that Anna had considerable problems with this English class. If she didn't get extra help she surely wouldn't pass, and even if she did she wouldn't have any of the skills necessary for Grade 9 English.

Mark had thought the parent conference would help to get things settled, but after talking to Anna's parents it became obvious that whatever Anna wanted, she got. They listened with sympathetic nods, and said they understood how frustrating she could be to talk to. But there was nothing they could suggest or do about it. They were very nice people who felt that it was essentially up to the school to educate Anna. They were blunt about having other issues to deal with beyond worrying about Anna's schoolwork.

The day after speaking to Anna's parents Mark talked to Nancy, the counsellor who worked with the Grade 8 girls. She said she wasn't sure what was going on, since Anna's name had come up several times already, but would get back to him in a couple of days.

The sealed envelope with "Confidential" marked on the outside certainly filled in a few blanks—but also made Mark wonder how he was going to get through to Anna.

After reading this memo please return it, and any attachments, in the enclosed envelope to:

   Nancy Elliott, Counsellor

To: Mark Whitman
Re: Anna Kelper
Date: Oct. 23, 1998

I've had a chance to review Anna's file and contact the counsellor at her elementary school. An assessment was done as part of the regular Grade 3 screening in that school. Anna's results on the Stanford Achievement Test (9th ed.) were in the average range, although reading, spelling, and thinking skills were just within the average cutoff limit (one to two points).

Based on these results the school-based team thought it would be advantageous to provide some extra teacher support on an "as needed" basis. No IEP was warranted, since it was felt that the teachers could adapt the regular curriculum to suit Anna's needs. The teachers' adapted materials have allowed Anna to progress through Grade 7.

With regard to her social/behaviour issues, there was confirmation that this behaviour wasn't new. Apparently Anna has caused considerable problems within the family. At this time the family is working with a counsellor. Anna was adopted as an infant and controls the family through the mother by saying they only adopted her to impress the neighbours. (The elementary teachers said that Anna usually added that the parents really didn't love her and that she wants to find her real mother. Apparently she'll say this to complete strangers.) Mrs. Kelper suffers from migraine headaches. Both parents appear to have very little control over Anna.

I've spoken to Dan Clark, the Vice-Principal, about this student. At this point the test results don't indicate the necessity for a mandatory IEP. We'd like to suggest that teachers adapt the curriculum for Anna, as was done in the elementary school. Several other teachers have commented on her behaviour, but it's not overt and hasn't resulted in any disciplinary action. The underlying issues appear to be a family matter, and unless they affect her schoolwork these should not be considered a problem.

Ministry of Education

Student Record Card

Intermediate

Family Name: <u>KELPER</u>
Given Names (first, middle):   <u>ANNA JUNE</u>
Birth Date (D/M/Y):   <u>11/08/85</u>

Achievement Record

(Average grade for year)

Subject	YEAR Grade 4	YEAR Grade 5	YEAR Grade 6	YEAR Grade 7
Language Arts	C	C-	C-	C-
Mathematics	C-	P	P	P
Social Studies	C+	C	C-	P
Science	C	C	C-	C-
Physical Education	B+	A-	B	B
French	C-	P	P	P
Fine Arts	A	B	B	B-
Music	B			

File 31

Frank

Jane Webster taught Grade 9 Science as well as Grade 11 Physics and Chemistry. Now that she'd been teaching for five years she felt that, for the most part, she had the curriculum and its variations organized. This small school had been a challenge to her ingenuity and creativity from the beginning. Its students came from a range of backgrounds, culturally as well as economically, and the large apartment block down the street was home to many of them. But there was a small segment of transient families who would stay for only about a year and then move on, often in the middle of the school year.

This constant moving frequently caused problems for students, especially if they were in need of some special assistance. Frank was one of these students. His family had moved into the neighbourhood over the Labour Day weekend, and he'd started school the following Monday, after the rest of her Grade 9 Science class had pretty much settled into a routine. He was a nice boy with wonderful manners. He had a great smile and seemed to have a number of skills in breaking the ice and making friends. (This was a bit unusual, since most adolescents don't like change and making new friends is often difficult for them.) By the time October came around Frank and two or three boys all hung around together. Jane had overheard some after-school plans, so she knew that he'd quickly settled into the neighbourhood.

But Grade 9 Science was becoming quite a challenge for Frank. Jane was concerned about his very low reading ability and the fact that he had great difficulty understanding some of the more basic concepts in Science. She'd put the students into working groups for labs and in-class activities, so she knew that Frank got some help with the reading. Unless the other boys helped, Frank used very simplistic sentence structures in his written work and the concepts were often wrong, even when the sentence and grammar problems were taken into consideration. By the second week in October Jane and a couple of Frank's other teachers went to speak to the counsellor.

The counsellor had just received the records on Frank, so this meeting with the teachers was timely. As was often the case, his permanent records were slow to show up—and even when they did there wasn't much in there. Frank's reports contained very little detailed information. Apparently he'd had some formal testing during elementary school, when the teachers noted the same discrepancies between his work and that considered grade-appropriate. Frank's reading scores were always two to three grade equivalents below his actual grade level. A group intelligence test given in Grade 4 put his IQ at 77; Frank's family had moved from that school district before the district school psychologist had an opportunity to test him further. In the next school it appeared that an informal evaluation had been done on his adaptive behaviours, and since no problems were found Frank wasn't designated as needing an IEP. From Grade 5 on, Frank relied on schools and teachers to adapt materials so that he could progress through elementary school.

Even with this small amount of information Jane and the other teachers thought the report accurately reflected Frank's academic ability. He had no adaptive problems, and if the IQ score was somewhat accurate then he fell within that grey area for services. Jane knew that definitional cutoffs (and recent funding problems) meant that Frank wouldn't be given a formal IEP.

The counsellor and teachers decided to undertake an informal education plan for Frank, a process that the school had formalized the year before. A sheet was to be filled out by each teacher, then at another meeting they would decide on a unified set of strategies so that the student would be reinforced in every class.

Each teacher would identify those specific areas where Frank was having trouble in class and offer some ideas for remediation. The goal was to give Frank coping tools that he could take with him if his family moved again. There was also the issue of providing a direction for him as he progressed through secondary school. While the Technical Studies teacher seemed to be the most important person for Frank's future skills training, all the teachers recognized the need for a unified support system.

Now came the hard part—filling out the sheet.

MEREDITH SECONDARY SCHOOL

COUNSELING OFFICE

INFORMAL EDUCATION PLAN WORKSHEET

Student _Frank Thomas_

Date _Oct. 4, 1999_

Grade _9_

Subject Area _Science_ Block _C_

Teacher _Jane Webster_

Within your subject area:

1. List your specific concerns.

A. BELOW GRADE LEVEL READING - Although Frank seems to have a good vocabulary. Uses words appropriately - can't explain ideas

B. Problems with concepts unless very simplistic concrete demonstrations. Sometimes the demonstrative is remembered but Frank can't put the concept to it.

C. MATH NEEDS TO BE CONCRETE. FRANK JUST "STOPS" WHEN CONFRONTED WITH ANYTHING MORE DIFFICULT THAN BASIC MATH.

2. Identify specific strengths.
   A. NICE PERSONALITY
   B. GOOD MANNERS
   C. MAKES FRIENDS EASILY
   D. WILLING TO TRY
   E. WORKS WELL WITH OTHER STUDENTS
      (WANTS TO DRIVE A CONCRETE TRUCK - HIS
      FAMILY WANTS HIM TO HAVE A H.S. DIPLOMA).

3. Identify specific areas for remediation or skills training.

4. List some ideas you feel might be useful to try.

5. List specific goals for this student.

File 32

Janet

Janet Wong had always loved to draw, and not only that, she was good at it. So Katie Warren could understand Janet's frustration about the fact that she might never realize her dream of further training at the local college.

Katie had been an art teacher at Davidson Creek Secondary School for eight years, and during that time she'd encountered several very talented students who'd gone on to complete various post-secondary programs in art. One young man even sent her a card at Christmas from Toronto, where he worked designing computer graphics for a highly successful company. He said that it was her encouragement that had inspired him to pursue his art career, and Katie figured it had been that comment that had made her watch Janet a bit more closely.

Janet was a very conscientious and hard-working person. It wasn't until Grade 11 that Katie had an opportunity to work closely with her, although Janet's artwork was well known since she often volunteered to make posters and help with designing decorations for school events. What Katie hadn't known was that Janet, while talented in art, was having extreme difficulty with her academic classes. Things had become progressively worse over the years, until now she was failing Grade 11 English and Social Studies. All this became evident when Katie asked Janet about the progress of her portfolio. Janet seemed embarrassed about even discussing the project, but finally admitted that she'd stopped working on it at Christmas. From this conversation Katie learned that Janet came from a more traditional Oriental home, where academics were highly valued. While Janet and her brother were born in Canada, her parents had retained many of the family traditions and values from their original home in China. Since her academics weren't even at a passing level her parents wanted her to spend more time and effort on those courses rather than on the art.

Katie understood all this, and also knew that it would probably be the same with most of the parents she knew. Academics were important, since they formed part of the requirements necessary to enter most post-secondary institutions. But at the same time Katie wanted to see Janet have a chance to continue to develop her artistic talent. Janet's portfolio would be part of that entrance requirement if she wanted to pursue a career in art. By the end of the day Katie had decided to talk to the counsellor to find out how to help Janet.

It took two days before Katie got the memo from counselling. She sat looking at Janet's sketchbook, re-reading the memo, and trying to figure out what she was going to do.

MEMO FROM COUNSELLING

RE: Janet Wong
Date: January 21, 1999

Katie,

Janet's name was already on my list of students to speak to about grades this term. Our conversation was a good addition to the small amount I have on file.

In general, Janet has had a reading problem throughout her school history. The standardized scores from Grade 6 (the last time they were done) indicate a word identification grade equivalent of 3.7 and a comprehension grade equivalent of 4.5. I suspect this reading problem is what's caused Janet so many difficulties in academics. I called Jon Case, the counsellor for the elementary school, who said that he'd tried several times to have Janet's reading evaluated in more detail. Her parents wouldn't agree to the testing, however, and so the elementary teachers worked with Janet by adapting materials, etc.

I spoke to Janet yesterday, since it had already been scheduled. She pointed out that her brother had helped her with the reading and her homework until he'd left for university this past September. Since her parents have limited written English she's had to do all the reading and homework on her own. I offered the help of the resource room and the teachers there, but Janet was adamant that she'd be labelled a "dummy" if she were to be seen going there for help.

After my resource room suggestion Janet lost interest in my help. Perhaps you might have some more ideas. I'd like to help, but Janet seems to have tuned me out. Please let me know what you decide.

Jan

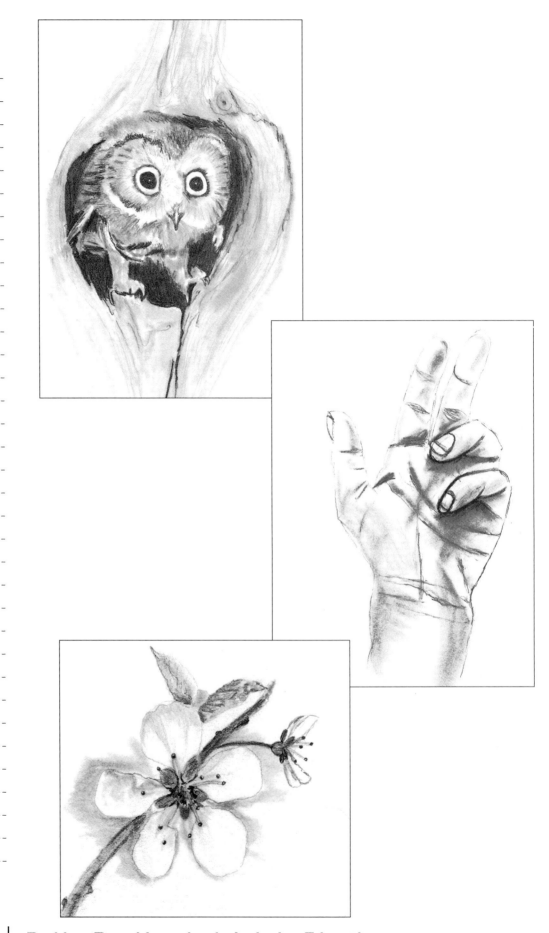

File 33

Mark

Students coming into the Middle School were always at a bit of a loss. The change from Grade 6 in an elementary school to this large building where hundreds of Grade 7s, 8s, and 9s noisily shuffled to different rooms always took its toll on the new students. However, almost every faculty member had specifically requested placement in this school. Since Bill's training in university was at the Middle School level he was prepared for the academic transition between the elementary and secondary curricula. He was also prepared for the social/emotional/maturational transitions that went along with becoming an adolescent. But what occupied his mind at the moment was Mark. Despite his one course in special education Bill wasn't really sure how to even begin teaching him English 7, Language Arts.

Mark was an average young adolescent with a wonderful sense of humour. He had several friends who hung around as a group and ate lunch together. Mark's exceptionally low vision didn't seem to be an issue with this group of boys. Bill had even observed an informal game of hoops where Mark had joined the lineup. He'd been given the ball, the boy behind him set up his angle, and when Mark missed his shot he returned to his place at the end of the line. No, social acceptance didn't seem to be a problem—it was academics that was the difficulty.

As well as his severe vision impairment Mark had several difficulties with motor skills resulting from a mild form of cerebral palsy. Apparently his elementary teachers, in conjunction with the itinerant teacher of students with visual impairments, had decided not to emphasize certain literacy tools requiring refined visual–motor skills such as handwriting, touch typing, and Braille reading. But now that Mark was heading for secondary school it became apparent that the previous methods were no longer enough. Just before the summer the school-based team asked the district to arrange an independent Learning Media Assessment at Mark's elementary school.

The principal had given each of Mark's teachers copies of the Learning Media Assessment. While the itinerant teacher of students with visual impairments would be available to assist Mark, each teacher had been asked to come to the meeting next week with specific ideas for their individual classes. Bill knew he had a long weekend ahead of him.

LEARNING MEDIA ASSESSMENT REPORT

Name:	Mark Sihota
Birth Date:	Feb. 1, 1987
Age:	12 years
Date of Evaluation:	May 26 and 27, 1999
Date of Report:	June 2, 1999
Grade:	6
Parents:	Ralph and Naz Sihota
Address:	1421 Franklin St.
	Brunswick Park, Alberta
Telephone:	555-3315

PURPOSE OF ASSESSMENT

The school district requested an independent learning media assessment to provide more comprehensive information on Mark's learning and literacy media needs.

ASSESSMENT STRATEGIES

- Observations in integrated Language Arts class and orientation and mobility lesson.
- Interview with parent, regular classroom teachers, resource room teacher, teacher of students with visual impairments, diagnostician, physical therapist, occupational therapy assistant.
- Direct assessment of reading efficiency in print, potential for Braille reading, and handwriting.
- Review of selected previous assessment results and other records.

ASSESSMENT RESULTS

Use of Sensory Channels

An objective procedure was used to document Mark's use of sensory channels in natural settings. He was observed on two occasions in Language Arts class and during an orientation and mobility lesson. Individual behaviours were recorded. For each behaviour, the examiner noted if Mark used visual, tactual, and/or auditory information; both primary and secondary sources of sensory information were noted. (See Form 2.)

Mark uses vision as the primary source for gathering sensory information and uses touch and hearing as secondary sources. It should be noted that this procedure documents the student's existing approach to tasks, and not necessarily the most efficient one. Mark uses the sensory channels he's been taught to use and has been reinforced for using.

Visual Functioning

Records indicated that Mark's left eye is anophthalmic and is fitted with a prosthesis. His right eye is microphthalmic with a cataract. His distance acuity is 10/140 (20/280) with correction, and his near acuity is 1M print at 2 cm. While glaucoma can accompany microphthalmia, there is no evidence of this to date. Available data suggests that his eye condition is stable. A recent low vision clinic report indicated that optical devices will not improve near visual functioning, but that his conventional spectacles should be worn for near work. Information on Mark's visual functioning indicates that there has not been a change in functioning that would directly affect his learning and literacy media.

Reading Efficiency

Objective data were collected on Mark's reading rate with comprehension, including both typical reading materials from an informal reading inventory (IRI) and content materials used in the classroom. Following is a summary of findings:

Type of Passage	Mode	Comprehension	Rate
Grade 3 from IRI (Form A)	Large Print	75%	45 wpm
Grade 4 from IRI (Form A)	Large Print	75%	41 wpm
Grade 4 from IRI (Form D)	Large Print	75%	44 wpm
Grade 4 from IRI (Form C)	CCTV	88%	41 wpm
Grade 4 from SRA (Brown Level)	Regular Print	Average	49 wpm
Grade 6 Science Book	Large Print	Average	38 wpm
Grade 6 Social Studies Book	Large Print	Average	48 wpm

The first source of data on reading efficiency was obtained with the Informal Reading Inventory by Burns and Roe. Mark was asked to read short passages ranging in length from 149 to 235 words and then to answer 8 to 10 comprehension questions. Print size ranged from 18 to 24 point type, so all passages were considered large print. One form of the test was administered late on Wednesday afternoon, and another form was administered mid-morning on Thursday.

For the purposes of calculating reading efficiency, only those passages were included in which Mark read with at least 75% comprehension. Reading efficiency rates were consistently found at around 45 words per minute. His working distance was from 1.5 to 2 inches, regardless of whether he wore his glasses. Results of the IRI indicated that Mark's instructional reading level was at Grade 2, and his frustration level was at Grade 3. However, a more accurate reading assessment instrument needs to be administered to pinpoint Mark's reading level more precisely.

Mark was given an opportunity to practise reading with the closed-circuit television on Wednesday afternoon, and was given a timed reading on Thursday morning. On Wednesday he was shown how to use the various controls and the tracking table. Initial observations indicated that he was able to scan words presented on the screen while moving the table with adequate motor control. He adjusted the letters to about 1 inch in height and read from a distance of 4 inches. Mark tended to pull the table toward himself to advance the reading material, rather than pushing it away from himself. This is common for students who are inexperienced in reading with the CCTV. On Thursday Mark demonstrated excellent recall on use of the controls, and he independently set them according to his preferences. Most notably, he demonstrated much more efficient use of the tracking table by appropriately pushing the table away from himself to advance the reading passage. On a timed reading Mark read a Grade 4 passage at 41 wpm with the CCTV with good comprehension. This reading rate is very similar to those obtained in large print. Mark demonstrated the motor skills necessary to read with the CCTV, and his efficiency will increase with repeated practice and experience.

Mark was also asked to read short passages (226 and 164 words) from the large print Science and Social Studies textbooks he uses in the classroom. To select a passage from his Science book Mark independently used the table of contents to locate a familiar passage on birds. He read this passage at 38 words per minute and then answered general comprehension questions prepared impromptu by the examiner. His level of comprehension was determined to be average through the examiner's judgment. In the Social Studies book Mark first answered several questions accurately about Canadian geography. For example, he stated that British Columbia was west of Alberta and that the Great Lakes were bordered by Canada and the United States. He then read a passage on natural resources in Alberta at a rate of 48 wpm with average comprehension.

On two occasions Mark was asked to read in regular print. He read a passage from the SRA reading series, printed in approximately 12 point type, at a rate of 49 wpm with adequate comprehension. On another occasion he was asked to read a paragraph from the regular print version of a Grade 6 Science worksheet. While no objective rate was taken, it was noted that Mark read fluently from a passage with poor contrast—black letters on a dark purple background—and responded to the content of the passage.

Several observations relative to reading efficiency are noteworthy. First, Mark appeared to deliberately select when to wear his glasses when reading. No dramatic difference was noted in reading efficiency when his glasses were on or off. Second, there was no appreciable difference in reading efficiency when Mark read in different sizes of print or with the CCTV. He used some strategies for independently adapting to different print sizes, such as adjusting his working distance and selecting when to use his glasses. Third, he generally tilted the materials he was reading. When asked if he would like to use a reading stand, Mark indicated that he would not.

Handwriting

According to information obtained during interviews, Mark uses keyboarding and dictation as his primary modes of expressive writing. Handwriting was not pursued as a primary mode of writing due to fine motor difficulties from the mild CP. However, he does use handwriting on a limited basis for completing computation problems in Math class.

As part of this assessment, Mark was asked to write the numbers from 1 to 10 and his name. It was observed that several numbers and letters did not conform to the standard formations, but rather were "drawn" to look like them. Given the satisfactory level of the fine motor control that was demonstrated, the examiner drew some primary-style lines (solid lines with a dashed line separating them) and then demonstrated a few letter formations for Mark to imitate. He did so with good accuracy (given no practice) and with direct attention to starting and stopping on the appropriate lines. Such excellent progress in a short instructional session strongly suggests Mark's potential for developing handwriting skills as an option for expressive communication.

Literacy Tools

At the current time Mark primarily uses large print for reading, with regular print used for some tasks. He uses live readers to an extent, but is not in purposeful control of the reading process. That is, he's not yet directing the live reader to read in a strategic manner. For writing he primarily uses keyboarding with a large-print word processing program and dictation to an adult for recording answers. He is currently receiving instruction in touch typing skills, but uses a hunt and peck method in the classroom. Objective data collected by the teacher indicates that he is roughly comparable in writing rates with the two methods, averaging around 15 to 17 words per minute. Handwriting is used sometimes for solving computation problems in Math, but is not used for general expressive writing.

Team members asked the examiner to assess Mark's potential for reading and writing in Braille. On both days of the assessment basic tracking and discrimination activities were presented. On Wednesday Mark demonstrated rough tracking movements across Braille lines, but was able to generally move from the top of the page to the bottom of the page with prompting. On Thursday he demonstrated more efficient tracking movement, so he was presented with two types of discrimination tasks. The first involved tracking lines of actual Braille that were interspersed with full cells, as visually illustrated in Braille Sample 1.

He was directed to track the lines and to indicate when he came to the full cell. Mark was able to complete this task with good accuracy while demonstrating satisfactory tracking skills. He showed some tendency to want to examine the Braille visually, but responded to prompts to only feel the lines. On the second discrimination task, he was presented with a page with sets of Braille symbols (Braille Sample 2) and was asked to indicate the symbol that was different. While he was able to maintain contact with the Braille symbols, Mark was not successful in completing the task. However, one would not be expected to complete such a task without adequate instruction, so this *does not* indicate in any way a lack of potential for Braille reading and writing. The level of success demonstrated in tracking and discrimination skills on the first Braille task sufficiently indicates the potential for developing Braille reading and writing skills if this is determined by the educational team to be a priority.

SUMMARY OF MAJOR FINDINGS

- Mark uses a combination of the visual, auditory, and tactual sensory channels for learning. Based on objective documentation, he demonstrated use of vision as the primary channel and use of hearing and touch as secondary channels.

- Oral reading rates with comprehension were approximately 45 words per minute on typical Grade 4 reading materials and Grade 6 Science and Social Studies passages.

- Mark has a limited repertoire of literacy tools for accomplishing reading and writing tasks. Primary reading options include large print and use of live readers. Primary writing options include keyboarding and dictation.

- Mark demonstrated the motor skills necessary to read with the CCTV and to write in manuscript. Furthermore, he demonstrated a rudimentary level of tracking skills and tactual sensitivity that may indicate his potential for learning to read and write Braille.

RECOMMENDATIONS

The following recommendations are offered to the educational team for their consideration in planning an appropriate educational program for Mark. It's imperative that all team members, including the parents and allied professionals, decide on the priorities for Mark and then provide the intensity of services required to address those prioritized needs. A clear focus and structure for the upcoming school year as Mark enters Middle School will ensure that all learning time is used to its maximum benefit.

1. *Expand literacy tools.* Mark needs a variety of options for completing reading and writing tasks. Given a full repertoire of literacy tools, he can then deliberately choose—with instruction and guidance—which option or options will allow the most efficient way to complete a given task. The following literacy tools should be among the options considered by the educational team:

Reading Tools

- increased use of regular print
- use of CCTV
- use of textbooks on tape
- directed use of a live reader
- use of Echo speech synthesizer and enlarged print on computer

Writing Tools

- use of manuscript writing
- extended use of touch typing and word processing with Echo and enlarged print on computer
- use of live writer (although limited)
- use of tape recorder for recording answers and notes

The focus of instruction should be placed on expanding options for completing literacy tasks, not limiting options. Reading regular print and using books on tape are valuable options for completing certain tasks. Mark needs to learn that some options are better for certain tasks than others, but he won't be in a position to make such decisions unless he has a range of options from which to select.

2. *Teach manuscript handwriting skills.* Mark does have the motor ability and the desire to learn handwriting skills. The educational team should consider this as a key priority in expanding Mark's writing options. He'll need primary-style writing paper (upper and lower solid lines with middle dotted line) with sharp contrast and consistent instruction to learn proper letter formations. Since he has been using some writing for Math, this may be the best area to focus on initially. He'll need to decrease the size of his writing over the upcoming years. For beginning instruction, line widths of about 1 or 1.25 inches will be appropriate.

3. *Teach touch typing skills.* The educational team has made a commitment to teach touch typing and this should continue and intensify. The hunt-and-peck method is not efficient for anyone, and is even less efficient for a student with low vision. Mark will need to continue using the hunt-and-peck method for some period of time until he gains sufficient touch typing skills, but a transition should begin as soon as possible to touch typing alone. He'll continue to benefit from auditory feedback provided by the Echo speech synthesizer, as well as the visual information from the enlarged print on the computer screen. The large letters on the keyboard should be faded and eventually eliminated as he increases his proficiency with touch typing.

4. *Teach use of the CCTV.* Mark has the motor ability now to make use of the CCTV as an option for reading. Actually, very little instruction will be needed as he has demonstrated the basic skills needed to use the CCTV. The focus should be placed on providing access to a CCTV and providing practice in its use. To gain efficiency, Mark will need extended practice in continuous text reading. He needs to learn that he can gain a more comfortable working distance and posture by increasing the size of the letters and moving back farther from the screen, as the same retinal image will be gained as with the closer working distance. Consultation with the OT/PT will help determine the best posture for reading.

5. *Consider the possible role of Braille reading and writing in Mark's repertoire of literacy tools.* Mark may have the potential to develop Braille reading and writing skills. However, the question is whether it's a priority need at this point,

and that question can be answered only by the educational team. If his eye condition remains stable and he develops other efficient options for reading and writing, I feel that Braille should be considered as a future option if the need arises. If his eye condition doesn't remain stable or if consistent and targeted instruction doesn't yield other efficient literacy tools, then Braille reading and writing instructions should be given deliberate consideration. If the decision is to introduce Braille reading and writing an intensive period of time must be set aside daily for instruction (such as 1 or 1.5 hours daily).

6. *Reconsider the need for abacus instruction.* I recommend placing emphasis on handwriting skills as an avenue for computation. While the abacus is an important option to consider for computation, developing efficiency and accuracy in its use is a long-term process. I feel Mark has other needs, such as those listed above, that take priority over abacus instruction. Also, I believe that computation on paper can become more efficient more quickly than use of the abacus. Computation on paper will, however, require consistent and intensive instruction.

7. *Use an experiential, multisensory approach to learning.* Mark has the ability to use all his senses for learning, and he should be given repeated exposure to meaningful experiences in real contexts for learning through all his sensory channels. According to his teacher, a multisensory approach was used throughout the previous school year, and this approach should continue. Students with low vision often miss valuable information because use of vision alone may provide inadequate or inaccurate information. A multisensory approach to learning alleviates much of this potential problem. Multisensory experiences must extend beyond the classroom and into the home and community. Using O&M lessons to provide age-appropriate experiences is a meaningful and practical approach for ensuring that Mark gains a wide variety of quality life experiences.

8. *Provide sufficient time and services to develop needed skills.* After the educational team has delineated and prioritized needed literacy tools and other skills an appropriate program should be developed to adequately meet those needs. The team may find that an integrated Middle School program will not provide sufficient time for intensive instruction. Therefore, a period of time may need to be devoted to specifically teaching compensatory skills in a more specialized environment. The rationale is that Mark would then have the repertoire of literacy tools and other skills to benefit meaningfully from an integrated school program. Regardless of the instructional arrangement, sufficient instructional time must be devoted to developing the specialized skills that Mark will need for independent living and employment.

9. *Provide continuing assessment.* Learning media assessment, as well as other assessment processes, are most meaningful when conducted on a continuing basis. Mark's needs have changed considerably over the past few years, and therefore the instructional program and strategies should change as well. Principles of diagnostic teaching should be used to continually assess emerging skills and changing needs. Thus, Mark will benefit from all learning experiences.

Marylou Ricker
Teacher of Students with Visual Impairments

BRAILLE READING SAMPLES

Sample 1

Sample 2

USE OF SENSORY CHANNELS

Student _Mark Sihata_
Setting/Activity _Language Arts Class and O&M Lesson_
Date _05/26/99_ Observer _Marylone Reiker_

Observed Behavior	Sensory Channel		
Class: Located desk	[V]	T	A
Reached for recorder	[V]	T	A
Placed disk in drive	[V]	T	A
Turned on computer (switch in back)	V	[T]	A
Switched on plug-in strip	[V]	(T)	A
Gathered papers together	[V]	T	A
Walked to teacher's desk	[V]	(T)	(A)
Glanced around room	[V]	T	A
Put on glasses	[V]	T	A
Looked at book	[V]	T	A
Took off glasses	V	[T]	A
Listened to teacher lecture	V	T	[A]
Stared at overhead light	[V]	T	A
	V	T	A
O & M: Identified parts of cane	[V]	(T)	A
Located office	[V]	T	A
Walked in straight line	[V]	T	A
Waved to friends in hall	[V]	T	A
Located office number	[V]	T	A
Turned corner	[V]	(T)	A
Looked behind along hall	[V]	T	A
Went to office door	[V]	T	A
Shook hands with teacher	[V]	(T)	A
Examined bulletin board	[V]	T	A
Located drinking fountain	[V]	T	A
	V	T	A

☐ Probable Primary Channel: _Visual_
◯ Probable Secondary Channel(s): _Tactual & auditory_

CONTINUING ASSESSMENT OF LITERACY MEDIA

Student _Mark Sihota_

Primary Reading Medium _Large Print_ Secondary Media _Live Readers_

Date _05/27/99_ Evaluator _Marylou Ricker_

Comments/Observations

Use of vision is considered a strength.

Additional Information on Visual Functioning

Is current information available from functional vision evaluations? Summarize.

Is current information available from ophthalmological examinations? Summarize.

Is current information available from clinical low vision evaluations? Summarize.

Does available information indicate a change in visual functioning? Yes (No)

_OD: Microphthalmia & cataract
Distance 10/140
Near: 14 print at 2 cm.
Field restriction to about 20° of fixation.
Normal intraocular pressure
Colour vision normal
OS: Anophthalmia – prosthesis
Wears glasses for near work.
Optical devices not helpful at near
Stable condition at present_

Reading Efficiency

Summarize the following information:

Current grade placement ___6___

Results of the _informal reading inventory_
(in student's primary reading medium)

	Grade	Rate
Independent level (≥90% comprehension)	3	45 wpm – used large print.
Instructional level (≥ 75% comprehension)	4	41–44 wpm – used large print.
Frustration level (<75% comprehension)	6	— used large print.

Reading of _content materials_ at grade placement

	Comp	Rate
Science	Ave.	38 wpm – used large print.
Social Studies	Ave.	48 wpm – used large print
Other: _____	—	—
_____	—	—

Does the student read with adequate comprehension? Yes (No) _Teachers indicate trouble with higher level comprehension._

Does the student read at a sufficient rate? Yes (No) _Literal recall OK._

Does the student read at a sufficient rate and with adequate comprehension in order to complete academic tasks with success? Yes (No)

_Other info: CCTV with Grade 4 passage: 41 wpm at 88% comprehension
Regular print with Grade 4 passage: 49 wpm and average comprehension._

Student *Mark Sikota*   Continuing Assessment of Literacy Media p.2

Academic Achievement

Is the student able to accomplish academic
tasks in the current medium/media with success?   Yes   No

Are time requirements to complete academic
tasks reasonable in comparison to peers without
visual impairments?   Yes   No

Information on academic achievement was gathered by a school psychologist and is not available at this time.

Handwriting

Is the student able to read his/her own
handwriting effectively?   Yes   (No)

Is handwriting a viable and effective *not enough*
mode of written communication? *info. cont. diagn. teaching*   Yes   No

Handwriting was not taught due to motor difficulties from mild CP.

Observations indicate potential to learn handwriting skills

Literacy Tools

Does the student have the repertoire of
literacy tools (such as sighted readers, slate and
stylus) to meet *current* educational needs?   Yes   (No)

Does the student have adequate skills in use
of technology to meet *current* educational needs?   (Yes)   No

Does the student have the repertoire of literacy
tools necessary to achieve *future* educational
and/or vocational goals?   Yes   (No)

Does the student have adequate skills in use
of technology to achieve *future* educational
and vocational goals?   Yes   (No)

Current options
Reading: lg. print and live readers
Writing: keyboarding (hunt & peck) and dictation
Uses computer with lg. print and Echo output

Factors to be considered by the educational team:

Recommendations: 1) Expand repertoire of literacy tools

    2) Teach manuscript writing skills

    3) Teach touch typing / keyboarding

    4) Teach use of CCTV

    5) Consider braille reading as a future option

File 34

Anson

Anson—there he was again, in a corner of the school grounds, playing by himself during recess while his Grade 2 classmates noisily and happily joined in games together and enjoyed the warm spring sun. Over the past six weeks Larissa Barnes, the classroom teacher of this rambunctious group, had noticed that Anson had increasingly preferred solitary play. She wasn't sure what to make of it. Anson had entered her classroom the previous September the same way most of her other students had: as an excited six-and-half-year-old with beginning reading skills, indicating good potential for the year ahead, and some baby-like speech, reminding Larissa that he was still really just a little boy. Larissa clearly recalled the morning in September when Anson proudly announced, "My muver bought me a wabbit!"

But as the year had progressed Anson's speech didn't improve, and Larissa, more concerned with some of her students whose special learning needs were quite pronounced, hadn't paid attention to this fact until Anson's solitary social behaviour became apparent. She *had* noticed some of the boys teasing Anson about his baby-like speech, and his mother had sent a note that morning indicating that Anson didn't like coming to school any more. Anson's academic performance was consistent and within expectations, although Larissa had noticed some surprising spelling errors recently. When Larissa had pointed out his speech difficulty to her vice-principal last week, she was assured that Anson would "outgrow the problem." The vice-principal had also informed her that the waiting list for an assessment by the district speech and language pathologist was very long, and that he'd support a referral only for well-documented or obvious cases. As a first-year teacher Larissa wished she had more experience behind her to guide her judgment in situations like this!

But the first step, it seemed to Larissa, was to consider if Anson really would outgrow this speech problem. What speech sounds *should* a seven-year-old have in place, anyway?

April 22, 1999 _____ Spelling _____ Anson

1. Story ✓ _____
2. inside ✓ _____
3. lake ✓
4. house ✓
5. blue ✓
6. spider ✓
7. wocket ✗ rocket
8. (A)apple ✓
9. weddy ✗ ready
10. fire ✓

Dear Mrs. Barnes,

Anson has been very upset at the thought of going to school lately. He says that the other children tease him and call him a baby.

I am very concerned about this. Could we meet as soon as possible to discuss this?

Marlene Stewart

File 35

Claire

It was the Friday before Labour Day, and Martin Johnson had spent the past three days poring over student files, sitting in staff meetings, and arranging his classroom. He felt ready to welcome the students who'd be forming his Grade 8 class next week—with one possible exception. Claire Bennett, a 14-year-old girl with a severe hearing loss in both ears, was transferring into this school district and would be joining Martin's class. In spite of being hard of hearing since birth, it seemed that Claire had been fully integrated into regular classrooms throughout elementary school. Prior to her departure from her previous school Claire's speech and language skills had been assessed by the district speech–language pathologist. Somehow that assessment report was the only document focussing specifically on Claire's unique learning needs to have followed her to this new placement.

Martin was sure that the report contained some helpful clues for supporting Claire's learning—but why did it seem so full of jargon? How could Martin use the information contained in the report to help him be an effective teacher for Claire?

SPEECH LANGUAGE ASSESSMENT REPORT

Name: Claire Bennett

School: Summercrest Elementary

Date: June 16, 1999

BACKGROUND INFORMATION

Claire Bennett is a Grade 8 student at Summercrest Elementary School. She wears hearing aids regularly at school and out of school. She communicates in spoken English and is easy to understand. She presented as a friendly, sociable young woman.

FOCUS OF THERAPY

Claire has not attended speech therapy so far this year. This decision was made in consultation with Claire, her parents, and the itinerant teacher of the deaf and hard of hearing, who monitored Claire's academic progress throughout the year and provided one-on-one tutoring. Although she's a capable student and works hard in therapy sessions, Claire indicated that she wanted a break from weekly speech–language intervention.

TESTING

Testing was completed in June at the request of the classroom teacher and the itinerant teacher of the deaf and hard of hearing.

TEST RESULTS

It's important to recognize that scores on all standardized tests, unless otherwise indicated, must be interpreted with caution as the normative data are based on typically hearing students. Scores serve as a baseline for future assessment, as a reference point for evaluating academic progress, and for setting speech and language goals.

The **Rhode Island Test of Language Structure (RITS)** was administered to evaluate understanding of English language structure. The **RITS** has been normed for hearing impaired subjects. Testing revealed that Claire's understanding of English language structure was normal for her age when compared to hearing impaired peers. The percentile score was 98.6% with a T-score of 71.9.

The **Clinical Evaluation of Language Fundamentals (3rd edition) (CLEF)** was designed to identify children, adolescents, and young adults who lack the basic foundations of language that characterize mature language use. In addition, it's used to supply information regarding a student's strengths and weaknesses in a range of language skills that focus on language form and content.

Claire's test scores on the **CLEF** were as follows:

	RAW SCORE	STANDARD SCORE	%ILE RANK
Receptive Language Scores			
Concepts and Directions	13	3	1
Word Classes	25	7	16
Semantic Relationships	9	4	2
Expressive Language Scores			
Formulated Sentences	19	3	1
Recalling Sentences	41	5	5
Sentence Assembly	15	8	25

Results indicated that Claire's knowledge of word classes and sentence assembly were within normal limits when compared to age-matched hearing peers. Weaknesses were demonstrated on the following subtests:

Concepts and Directions: This subtest assesses the ability to interpret, recall, and execute oral commands of increasing length and complexity that contain concepts requiring logical operations.

Semantic Relationships: This subtest assesses interpretation of semantic relationships in sentences (e.g., "A man is bigger than a: house, button, spoon, plane").

Formulated Sentences: This subtest assesses formulation of simple, compound, and complex sentences.

Recalling Sentences: This subtest assesses recall and reproduction of sentence surface structure as a function of syntactic complexity (e.g., "The truck was followed by the bus." —Repeat exactly as presented).

The **Adolescent Test of Problem Solving (TOPS)** was administered to test language-based critical thinking skills using logic and experience. Questions that focus on a broad range of critical thinking skills, including clarifying, analyzing, generating solutions, evaluating, and affective thinking, are included in the test. The test addresses the school curricula and the social arena faced by adolescents.

Test results revealed the following:

Raw Score	20
Age Equivalency	below norms
Percentile Rank	1
Standard Score	61

The results of this test revealed a severe delay in the area of language-based critical thinking skills when compared to age-matched hearing peers. Claire scored 2.5 standard deviations below the mean.

The **Goldman-Fristoe Test of Articulation** was administered to evaluate speech sound production. Test results revealed the following sound substitutions, omissions, and distortions at the word level:

TARGET	INITIAL	MEDIAL	FINAL
F			V
NG			D
T			K
CH	SH	SH	T
R			DIS*
S	D	D	/*
Z	D		
SKW	SHKW		
SL	SHL		
TR	TW		

*DIS=distortion
/=omission

All other speech sounds were pronounced correctly at the word level. Claire's conversational speech can be characterized as intelligible but noticeably in error.

CONCLUSIONS AND RECOMMENDATIONS

Claire's language abilities are delayed when compared to hearing peers. She could benefit from continued work in these areas of language. In addition, she could benefit from the use of the Speech Viewer Program at school (during her resource blocks or after school) to help her learn to monitor and correct her own speech errors.

It is recommended that:

1. Claire use the Speech Viewer Program while at school to increase speech sound production accuracy.

2. In collaboration with Claire's classroom teachers, a plan be developed to address language goals that will be incorporated into the classroom curriculum.

A. McCormick

Alexander McCormick, M.A., CCC-S-LP(c)
Certified Speech Language Pathologist

Bibliography

Bruner, J.S. (1960). *The process of education.* Cambridge, MA: Harvard University Press.

Boud, D. & Feletti, G. (1991). *The challenge of problem-based learning.* New York: St. Martins.

Chi, M., Glaser, R., & Farr, M.J. (Eds.) (1988). *The nature of expertise.* Hillsdale, NJ: Lawrence Erlbaum Associates.

Dewey, J. (1933). *How we think: A restatement of the relation of reflective thinking to the education process.* Lexington, MA: D.C. Heath.

Fogarty, R. (1997). *Problem-based learning and other curriculum models for the multiple intelligences classroom.* Arlington Heights, IL:IRI/Skylight Training and Publishing, Inc.

Fosnot, C.T. (Ed.) (1996). *Constructivism: Theory, perspectives, and practice.* New York: Teachers College Press.

Gallagher, S.A. (1997). Problem-based learning: Where did it come from, what does it do, and where is it going? *Journal for the Educaton of the Gifted, 20* (4), 332–362.

Gijselaers, W.H. (1996). Connecting problem-based practices with educational theory. In L. Wilkerson and W.M. Gijselaers (Eds.), *Bringing problem-based learning to higher education: Theory and practice.,* No. 68, Win., (13–21). San Francisco: Jossey-Bass Publishers.

Glasgow, N.A. (1997). *New curriculum for new times: A guide for student-centered, problem-based learning.* Thousand Oaks, CA: Corwin Press, Inc.

Koenig, A.J. & Holbrook, M.C. (1993). *Learning media assessment: A resource guide for teachers.* Austin, TX: Texas School for the Blind and Visually Impaired.

McKee, W. (1995). *Step-by-step problem-solving learning and behavior problems.* Unpublished manuscript, University of British Columbia.

Newmann, F.M. & Wehlage, G.C. (1993). Five standards of authentic instruction. *Educational Leadership, 50* (7), 8–12.

Sage, S.M. & Torp, L.T. (1997). What does it take to become a teacher of problem-based learning? *Journal of Staff Development, 18* (4) 32–38.

Savery, J.R. & Duffy, T.M. (1995). Problem-based learning: An instructional model and its constructivist framework. *Educational Technology, 35* (5), 31–38.

Stepien, W. & Gallagher, S. (1993). Problem-based learning: As authentic as it gets. *Educational Leadership, 50* (7), 25–29.

Voss, J.F. & Post, T.A. (1988). On solving of ill-structured problems. In M. Chi, R. Glaser & M.J. Farr (Eds.), *The nature of expertise.* Hillsdale, NJ: Lawrence Erlbaum Associates.

Wagner, R.K. & Sternberg, R.J. (1986). Tacit knowledge and intelligence in the everyday world. In R.J. Sternberg & R.K. Wagner (Eds.), *Practical intelligence: Nature and origins of competence in the everyday world.* Cambridge: Cambridge University Press.

Wilkerson, L. (1996). Tutors and small groups in problem-based learning: Lessons from the literature. In L. Wilkerson & W.H. Gijselaers (Eds.), *Bringing problem-based learning to higher education: Theory and practice.* No. 68, Win., San Francisco, CA: Jossey-Bass Publishers.

Voss, J.F. & Post, T.A. (1988). On the solving of ill-structured problems. In M. Chi, R. Glaser & M.J. Farr (Eds.), *The nature of expertise,* Hillsdale, NJ: Lawrence Erlbaum Associates.

Test References

Bracken, B.A. (1984). *Bracken Basic Concept Scale.* San Antonio, TX: The Psychological Corporation, Harcourt Brace & Co.

Brigance, A. (1991). *Revised Brigance Diagnostic Inventory of Early Development.* North Billerica, MA: Curriculum Associates, Inc.

Dunn,, L.M., & Dunn, L.M. (1981). *Peabody Picture Vocabulary Test—Revised.* Circle Pines, MN: American Guidance Service.

Dunn, L.M., & Markwardt, F.C. (1990). *Peabody Individual Achievement Test—Revised.* Circle Pines, MN: American Guidance Service.

Gresham, F.M., & Elliott, S.N. (1990). *Social Skills Rating System.* Circle Pines, MN: American Guidance Service.

Harter, S. (1985). *Self-Perception Profile for Children.* Unpublished test, University of Denver.

Kaufman. A.S., & Kaufman, N.L. (1983). *Kaufman Assessment Battery for Children.* Circle Pines, MN: American Guidance Service.

Kaufman, A. S., & Kaufman, N.L. (1985). *Kaufman Test of Educational Achievement.* Circle Pines, MN: American Guidance Service.

Sparrow, S.S., Balla, D.A., & Cicchetti, D.V. (1984). *Vineland Adaptive Behavior Scales.* Circle Pines, MN: American Guidance Service.

Thorndike, R.L., Hagen, E.P., & Sattler, J.M. (1986). *Stanford-Binet Intelligence Scale: Fourth Edition.* Chicago: Riverside Publishing.

Wechsler, D. (1991). *Wechsler Intelligence Scale for Children—Third Edition.* San Antonio: The Psychological Corporation.

Woodcock, R.W., & Johnson, M.B. (1989). *Woodcock-Johnson Psychoeducational Battery—Revised.* Chicago: Riverside Publishing.

Suggested Sample Web Sites

The number and variety of Web sites available precludes any comprehensive listing. As more specific sites are encountered during research they should be listed below in the space provided. This will provide a personalized Web listing.

Canadian Association of Speech–Language Pathologists and Audiologists
www.casslpa.ca/
Association for the Neurologically Disabled of Canada **www.AND.ca/**
Attention Deficit Disorder Library **qlink.queensu.ca/~3dwl8/add.htm**
Canadian Child Care Federation **www.cfc-efc.ca/cccf**
Canadian Charter of Rights and Freedoms **www.colba.net/~mgelinas/chrt/**
Canadian Down Syndrome Society **home.ican.net/~cdss/index.html**
Canadian Hearing Society **www.chs.ca/**
Canadian Institute of Child Health (CICH) **www.cich.ca/**
Canadian National Institute for the Blind **www.cnib.ca/**
Council for Exceptional Children **www.cec.sped.org/**
Disabled Peoples' International **www.escape.ca/~dppi/**
Internet Special Education Resources **wwww//iser.com/index.shtml**
Links to Learning Differences & Disabilities **www.vvcy.edu/aelweb/ldlnks.htm**
University of Delaware **www.udel.edu/pbl/**

Some Suggested Journals on Special Education

American Annals of the Deaf
British Journal of Special Education
B.C. Journal of Special Education
Canadian Journal of Special Education
Education and Training in Mental Retardation and Developmental Disabilities
Re:View (formerly *Education of the Visually Handicapped*)
Exceptional Children
Exceptional Parent
Exceptionality
Exceptionality Education Canada
Gifted Child Quarterly
Gifted Child Today (formerly *G/C/T*)
Gifted International
High Ability Studies
Imagine (education of highly able teenagers)
Intervention in School and Clinic
Journal for the Education of the Gifted
Journal of Autism and Childhood Schizophrenia
Journal of Autism and Developmental Disorders
Journal of Deaf Studies and Deaf Education
Journal of Educational and Psychological Consultation
Journal of Learning Disabilities
Journal of Secondary Gifted Education
The Journal of Special Education
Journal of Early Intervention
Journal of Visual Impairment and Blindness
Language, Speech and Hearing Services in Schools
Learning Disabilities Research and Practice
Perspectives in Education and Deafness
Preventing School Failure
Remedial and Special Education
Roeper Review (articles on education of highly able children)
School Psychology Quarterly
Teaching Exceptional Children
Topics in Early Childhood Special Education
The ACEHI Journal
The Volta Review (articles on learners who are deaf and hard of hearing)

Credits

Page 7, Step-By-Step Problem Solving: with thanks to Dr. William McKee of UBC.

Page 20, line drawing: with thanks to Meghan Porath.

Page 22, pot of gold story from Porath, M. (1996). Narrative performance in verbally gifted children. *Journal for the Education of the Gifted, 19* (3), p. 285. Reprinted by permission of the Journal for the Education of the Gifted.

Page 22, Fire Poem: with thanks to Camille Calloway Dinesen, age 5.

Page 38 and 40, line drawing: with thanks to Iona Wray.

Page 42, space academy story and prehistoric story: with thanks to Aaron Livingstone.

Page 46, Parent Profile Form: courtesy of John Robert Esliger.

Page 47, Student Profile Form: with thanks to Hannah Barclay. Form courtesy of John Robert Esliger.

Page 64, line drawing: with thanks to Travis Page.

Page 65, books log: with thanks to Travis Page.

Page 70, Counsellor Meeting Request Form: with thanks to John Robert Esliger.

Page 78, line drawing: with thanks to Meghan Porath.

Page 80, Seizure Observation Form: with thanks to A. John Jordan.

Page 95, Oral Reading Assignment Form: categories for oral reading assessment adapted from J.M. Sattler, (1992). *Assessment of children* (3rd edition). San Diego: Jerome M. Sattler Publisher, Inc.

Page 102, Writing Assignment: with thanks to Jacqueline Kupu.

Pages 116–122, Learning Media Report: with thanks to M. Cay Holbrook.

Page 125, Kwakwala terminology: with thanks to Audrey Wilson, T'lisalagi'lakw School, Alert Bay, British Columbia.

Page 125, Dogrib terminology: with thanks to Dr. Art More and the Dogrib Divisional School Board.

Page 126, writing assignments: with thanks to Tristan Jordan.

Pages 132–133, Informal Education Plan Worksheet: with thanks to A. Jordan.

Page 136, line drawings: original drawing by Anne C. Page.

Page 149, spelling test: with thanks to Daniel Asch.